Where Angels Fear to Tread

Where Angels Fear to Tread:
An Exploration of having Conversations
about Suicide in a Counselling Context

By

Susan Dale

Where Angels Fear to Tread:
An Exploration of having Conversations about Suicide in a Counselling Context,
by Susan Dale

This book first published 2010

Cambridge Scholars Publishing

12 Back Chapman Street, Newcastle upon Tyne, NE6 2XX, UK

British Library Cataloguing in Publication Data
A catalogue record for this book is available from the British Library

ISBN (10): 1-4438-2070-9, ISBN (13): 978-1-4438-2070-7

This book is dedicated to Alex,
and all of those people I have worked with
who have despaired of life itself.

TABLE OF CONTENTS

Foreword xi
Tim Bond

Acknowledgements xiii

Prologue... xv

Introduction 1
How to read this book
Terminology
Writing stories from the counselling room

Part 1: Narrative Begininnings

Chapter One.. 9
Using Narrative Practices to Co-research the Experience
of a Therapeutic Relationship
Alex: Journal December 2009
Introduction
Narrative as a social construction of lived experience
Reflexivity in counselling research
The interface between counselling and research
Narrative ethics when writing other peoples stories

Chapter Two.. 25
Suicidal Thoughts in the Counselling Room
Introduction
Client and counsellor perspectives regarding suicide
Professional responsibilities and accountability
Client rights and responsibilities
Ethics and dilemmas when researching with suicidal clients

Chapter Three 39
Introducing Alex
    Introduction
    A counsellors first impression
    Power control and knowledge
    Conversations with Alex December 2009
    Using narrative practices to side-step traditional structures of power
    and to explore the particularities of lived experience

Chapter Four 53
Narratively Speaking
    Introduction
    The beginnings of a research project
    Email conversations with Alex December 2004-January 2005
    Doing the research: turning conversation into text
    Introduction to the narratives

Part 2: Engaging with Suicide: The Narratives

Chapter Five 67
Dawn
    Introduction
    Alex: February-April 2000
    Email conversations about research January-March 2005

Chapter Six 89
Midday
    Introduction
    Email conversations about research March 2005
    Alex: May-June 2000
    Email conversations about research April 2005
    Alex: June-September 2000
    Email conversations about research April 2005

Chapter Seven.. 117
Evening
    Introduction
    Alex: October 2000-March 2001
    Email conversations about research April 2005
    Alex March-April 2001
    Email conversations about research April 2005

Part 3: Engaging with Life

Chapter Eight... 131
Night
    Introduction
    Email conversations with Alex May 2005
    Definitional Ceremony May 2005
    Email conversations with Alex June 2005

Chapter Nine.. 149
The Researchers Story
    Introduction
    Journal November 2004-April 2005
    Where am I now?

Chapter Ten 155
Endings and New Beginnings
    Introduction
    Email conversations with Alex February-March 2006
    Personal and professional learning from the research
    Suicide prevention stragegies that promote autonomy?
    The last word goes to Alex

Bibliography... 169

Index... 177

FOREWORD

Few topics challenge us more as therapists than working with suicidal clients. We are engaged in working with someone experiencing an intensity of emotional suffering that makes life seem unsustainable and undesirable. Traditional case studies tend to understate the lived experience of this encounter from both the therapist's and client's point of view. This book by Susan Dale is distinctive in its attention to lived experience of both client and counsellor and carefully considering the narrative research methods she uses to achieve this.

As I read the book, I was reminded of both the intensity of the "downs" for both client and therapist in this work and the courage both require to face these moments as someone faces the intensity of personal anguish. In my experience, words and the quality relationship seem quite fragile in the face of such profound despair when someone is contemplating the ending life. However these seemingly fragile tools can build the metaphorical hawsers by which both people are transformed within the therapeutic relationship. These abstract words seem empty in comparison to the richness of experience that this book communicates. We are invited to share the intensity of the struggle in which Susan and her client, Alex, are engaged and how, through the struggle, hope in the possibility of living emerges. This is book I would offer to any therapist, especially trainees, to prepare them for working about issues of suicide and suicidal intent.

This book will also be interest to researchers who are looking for examples of collaborative research within a narrative methodology. The careful attention to the ethical dimensions of the collaboration and care with which some things are shared with us as readers or explicitly concealed demonstrates how this type of research can be undertaken with integrity and respect. The quality of communicating both peoples' experiences is enhanced by commentaries developed through email exchanges. The simplicity of this device adds to the sense of authenticity. I would offer this book to any research student considering narrative research or how to be a collaborative researcher.

Working with suicidal clients is seldom straightforward or routine. Both therapist and client are staring into the void of imminent death and involved in the search for what makes life meaningful and what makes life sustainable. The therapist needs to do this to be sufficiently robust to contain the therapeutic relationship whilst the client decides a course of action to abandon living or to transform living into something more endurable in the hope that it might eventually become more than this. This book takes to the heart of this encounter, its challenges, and possibilities.

—Tim Bond
University of Bristol

Note

Tim Bond is a Professorial Teaching Fellow at the University of Bristol specialising on counselling, professional ethics and research methodology. He has written extensively about these topics. He is committed to applying the insights of counselling to his role as a leader and manager in the university, where he is currently a Head of School, and in a small practice of counselling and supervision.

ACKNOWLEDGEMENTS

There are so many people that have made the writing of this book possible, but I want to especially thank:

Alex. Without your courage and commitment, this book would never have been written.

Tim. For your encouragement and support and for believing I could write!

All of the tutors on the MSc Counselling programme, who were patient with a reluctant academic.

My counselling supervisors, Colin (who is still missed) Jan who is much appreciated, and Elyan who I am just getting to know. Without supervision counselling is nothing but words.

All participants who took part in the definitional ceremony. I have not named you, but you know who you are. Thank you so much for being there and contributing so richly

My family, Rebekah for your love, and the tea, flapjacks and brownies which sustained me. during the writing, John for always being there for me, and supporting me in both my research my work as a counsellor and my writing (Correcting my appalling spelling and grammar has been a time consuming task!). Adam and Sam who support their aged mother in so many ways and who have ensured she is computer literate.

PROLOGUE

Session Notes January 28th 2000

Session Notes January 28th 2000

I saw Alex (pseudonym) for the first time today, he is 35, and has self-referred because he is "desperate, and this is a last ditch attempt at trying to live".

He tells me that since his wife left him some eighteen months ago he has made ten suicide attempts which have resulted in him being admitted to hospital. "I don't know why I'm still alive, I've tried everything not to be" he says. Checking with his GP I find that the mental health team have discharged him saying he had no "diagnosable mental health condition" and that he is just "a time waster". He has decided that since he has "failed at suicide" he has to find a way of dealing with "all the crap that is going on in my head".

I feel sad, and at the same time amazed. So many times over the last few years I have heard similar stories, what is going on here?

INTRODUCTION

My interest in researching "what is going on" in conversations about suicide has developed over the last two decades due to the increasing number of referrals for counselling from people (mainly men) who like Alex reported using suicidal thoughts and behaviours to cope with extreme emotional pain. I have become more and more curious both about the way in which suicidal behaviour and thoughts are used by these people, and also the effect these behaviours have on the therapeutic relationship and on me as a counsellor.

During counselling training I completed two small studies exploring the ethical dilemmas posed when working with this client group (Dale 2003, 1999) and started to run training sessions for counsellors who reported feeling "de-skilled" and "terrified" when working with clients who reported suicidal intent.

I wanted to understand more about "what was going on" in these conversations, so when the opportunity arose, I used the academic requirements of Bristol University's MSc programme in counselling to explore more fully just how I could research the experience of these conversations (Dale 2006) and subsequently decided to develop a narrative inquiry for this purpose. The narratives emerging from this study form the backbone of this book, and provide a glimpse into the unique lived experience of two people who have had conversations about suicide in both counselling and research settings and include reflections over a period of ten years.

Etherington refers to her own writing from narrative perspectives as "reflections upon reflections upon reflections" (Etherington 2000:13) and this idea really resonates. As Alex and I sat down in a small coffee shop in Cardiff, in December 2009, to talk about turning the study into a book I was aware of layer upon layer of reflection, and how our stories from the counselling room have been overlaid with stories emerging from the research process, and now from the writing of a book. The narratives are constantly re-woven and added to over time and our sharing with other people. Rather than the narratives just being a record of data collected and giving a glimpse of pre-existing identities they show a process of social construction of lived experience, and the book aims to "show" these processes of research, rather than to "tell about" a research process that has happened.

With such a dynamic process, and so many layers of story, it has been difficult to know how to present words on a page that will enable the narratives to speak for themselves, but also enable academic and professional discussion relating to both the subject matter (having conversations about suicide in a counselling context) and also about the process and relevance of conducting this kind of research. The book is therefore split into three parts.

Part One entitled "**Narrative beginnings**" explores the use of narrative as a research tool, the interface between research and counselling, and the ethical and also professional responsibilities of counsellors working with suicidal clients and introduces Alex my co-researcher. Chapter 1 "Using narrative practices to co-research the experience of a therapeutic relationship" explores the concept of narrative as a social construction of lived experience, and what this might mean with regard to reflexivity, ethics, using a narrative research methodology and the interface between research and counselling. Chapter 2 "Suicidal thoughts in the counselling room" introduces both client and counsellor perspectives on having conversations about suicide in a counselling context exploring both professional rights and responsibilities alongside the rights and needs of clients highlighting some of the ethical challenges and dilemmas when working within counselling and research relationships. Chapter 3 "Introducing Alex" introduces Alex and explores moving from a counselling to research relationship, the use of narratives to explore the particularities of lived experience, and how the dynamics of power control and autonomy are negotiated. Chapter 4 "Narratively speaking" contains conversations with Alex about the research and shows the start of the research process and also gives an introduction to the narrative text.

Part 2 entitled, "**Engaging with suicide-the narratives**" uses the metaphor of a day's cycle to explore both the therapeutic, and research processes through the medium of a narrative and tell Alex's story of using suicide as a way of coping with extreme psychological pain. Chapter 5 "Dawn" Alex explores starting points and memories that have triggered his suicidal thoughts, feelings, and behaviours. Chapter 6 "Midday" explores the emergence of active suicidal thoughts and behaviours in the counselling room. Chapter 7 "Evening" explores how Alex and I found creative ways of working together and how he finds some alternative richer thicker descriptions of his life experience.

Part 3 entitled, **"Engaging with life"** shows how the process of counselling and research has enabled Alex to engage with life. Chapter 8 "Night" explores linking lives around the shared theme of suicidal through the use of a "definitional ceremony". This is a metaphor first described by anthropologist Barbara Myerhoff (1986; 1979) in her work with an elderly Jewish community in Los-Angeles, and later developed by narrative therapists such as White and Epston (2000; 1990) to enable people to re-connect and re-author their lives. Chapter 9 "The researcher's story" gives personal reflections on the research process. Chapter 10 "Endings and new beginnings" engages Alex in conversation about his experience of the research process, and explores how suicide prevention strategies can be developed that promote autonomy, and offers some conclusions, findings and new beginnings

How to read this book?

The book is ordered in the way in which I think would be helpful to the reader, but it may be that you would prefer to read, the narratives before (or even instead of) reading about the research process, or you may, like my husband, be someone who likes to read the ending before being troubled by the storyline! You are invited to start reading at whichever point suits you. I have tried to make each part self-explanatory in its own right.

Terminology

I have used the terms counselling, therapy, and psychotherapy interchangeably to mean a therapeutic undertaking agreed upon by someone who is commonly called a client and someone who is called counsellor, therapist, or psychotherapist.

Writing stories from the counselling room

One of the first jokes my son learnt at school which amused him so much that he would roll over and over on the floor convulsed with mirth was, "How do you know you have had an elephant in the fridge?" Answer:

"You can see his footprints in the butter". Being curious about why he found this so amusing I asked him to explain it to me. "Well" he said, "I should think it would be difficult to find the fridge let alone the butter with footprints in it. If you had an elephant in your kitchen the whole place would be wrecked. The joke writer is just pretending it wouldn't be".

"How has this got anything to do with conducting research about counselling?" I hear you ask. Well, I suppose as a counsellor what I feared most about conducting research with an ex-client, and trying to explore something of the experience of our conversations, especially conversations about something as emotive as suicide, was that the process of creating those footprints would wreck and destroy anything that the counselling relationship achieved.

Would it be possible to tell stories from the counselling room in ways that were a "celebration and extension of the therapeutic process" (Etherington 2001). I will leave you the reader to judge for yourself. Alex emailed me regarding the proposal to write this book saying:

From: Alex4research
Sent: 12 Nov 2009 17:08

Hi lol,
Yes the book sounds brilliant idea. Go with it.
My life is good now. It was so good to meet with you again, and for you to also meet (name) and of course our daughter (who enjoyed her 2nd birthday last week). Working as a drugs and alcohol counsellor I often find myself with folks who have given up on life. I understand much more now how it was for you then, and when I feel like walking away I remember your dogged determination not to let go whatever I threw at you and I stay although sometimes I wonder why you stayed and how you managed to persuade the NHS to let us have so many sessions!

Looking back I'm not sure whether it was the counselling or seeing those poems of my life which brought me back from the brink. I think probably I needed both, the counselling enabled me to talk and the project gave me a voice. Now I'm using my voice (and my ears) and even my brain (amazing that it wasn't curdled with the booze) to listen to others and stay with them, so it kind of goes round a full cycle.

I'm glad that these stories are not going to be wasted and that other people can learn from our experiences. Alex will always be part of who I am, and actually I'm quite proud of him-what is written won't take anything away from me, in fact it will give me a sense of achievement if only one person reads it and says "perhaps life is worth living" or a counsellor says "perhaps I can work with her or him".

I trust you absolutely. You can use whatever you like that we have written together with my blessing!

Let me have a copy of the book when it is finished and I'll use it to prop up the sideboard (only kidding)!

Thanks lol. Alex

PART 1:

NARRATIVE BEGINNINGS

CHAPTER ONE

USING NARRATIVE PRACTICES
TO CO-RESEARCH THE EXPERIENCE
OF A THERAPEUTIC RELATIONSHIP

Alex: Journal December 2009

Putting the chaos into stories
and having this witnessed.
I can never fully explain what that meant to me.

Allowing someone to see me for a moment.
Staying with me in the fear of that
'til I could learn to breathe again.
'til I could move.

Before,
caught in the headlights like a rabbit
psychiatric care meant
I was frozen.
Unable to move.
In the wrong.
About to get crushed.
Juggernauts of rules and wrong thinking labels passing too close
mind numbing drugs that held the chaos in.
One step and it would be over.
Putting the stories onto paper
was another thing; the next stage I think.
like a moving from a slow walk to a run.

Running well with the wind in my hair.
I could look at the stories again from a distance
and forgive that little kid.
Hold him even.
Use the stories to help others.
Writing them down
writing myself a different fate

Introduction

Therapeutic relationships are essentially private and confidential by their nature. If however we as counsellors and psychotherapists are to comply with the need for, evidence based practice and to understand what "works" when we are with our clients, and how our own processes impact on our work, we need to understand not just our client's processes but our own and the dynamic of relating to each other.

To explore these particularities of lived experience I wanted to use a methodology that was congruent with my views on how people make sense of their lives and my practice as a counsellor. As a counsellor I do not "do" counselling with my clients, rather I engage with them in a relationship in order to explore their world, and through this relationship I consider the client to be empowered to construct a "preferred reality" (Freedman and Combs 1996). In other words I see identity as socially constructed through relationship and the stories we tell of our life, meaning that there are always possibilities that we can change who we are and we can find richer thicker descriptions of our life.

Within this chapter I will explore the concept of narrative as a social construction of lived experience, reflexivity, the interface between counselling and research, and the ethical challenges faced when writing other people's stories.

Narrative as a social construction of lived experience

This section seems incredibly difficult to write. Words come and go and slip illusively through my fingers. I type a paragraph and then drift off track. "Narrative as a social construction of lived experience" seemed like a good enough heading and important for the reader to locate the forthcoming narrative text within a methodological framework and context. But, how to do that? What do I mean by narrative as a social construction of lived experience? Perhaps the answer is to tell the story of my involvement with these ideas.

Training as a counsellor in my thirties was my first dip into further education. As a young person leaving school, at sixteen, I had little or no academic aspirations except perhaps the love of a good book or story!

Models of how we become and develop Erikson (1982) Rayner (1986) were absorbed together with attachment theories Bowlby (1982) Howe, Brandon et al. (1999) and the idea that within all of us we have a "real" self Maslow (1973; 1968) Rowan (1983), that could be found by excavating through the layers of our experiences. I learnt also about offering a relationship to others that had core conditions of unconditional positive regard, acceptance, and empathy and how this enabled people to actualise and grow and become Rogers (1961) and to live lives they experienced as more fulfilling.

These ideas were for me like the rains after a serious drought. I absorbed them rapidly and tried to tie them up with my work as a counsellor. Within my own life I was able to explore my own inner world and I could make sense of most or all of these theories about self-development and identity. People continued to talk to me, tell me stories of their lives and I continued to learn new skills of counselling. Psychodynamic theories Jacobs (1998) intermingled with humanistic core conditions, cognitive behavioural theories Trowner, Casey et al. (1988) of linking thoughts feelings and behaviours became a way of giving people skills to cope with difficult life experiences. Neuro Linguistic Programming (NLP) O'Connor and Seymour (1995) helped me study the way people stored memories, and how childhood trauma could be overcome. Metaphor therapy and clean language and hypnosis Grove and Panzer (1991) all added to the expanding "toolkit". I learnt about the effects of trauma, childhood abuse and neglect, how alcohol, drugs and sometimes even self-harm were used to help people "feel" better and more in control.

I could see that aspects of all of these theories rang true for some people, and that there was something about the way people told their stories to me that changed their experiences. But there still felt something missing from my understanding. Then one day Jane[1] a tutor on the MSc counselling course said something that made the hairs on the back of my neck stand on end. I wrote it in my notebook. I didn't understand fully what she meant, but I knew that with these words all my learning and understandings that had been the cornerstones of my therapeutic practice were crumbling, and that they had to crumble in order for new cornerstones which were somehow much more fluid, but at the same time firmer.

Journal October 1999
All I can remember of the whole day are these words and they have shaken me. Everything about me feels shaken, stirred and I am afraid, yet excited. Jane: "of course the theories underpinning most psychological therapies come with a structuralist understanding of self. They see 'self' as a construct that can be excavated, found, studied, and reported on. But, there is another view coming from a post-structuralist perspective. This view considers the 'self' to be created through relationship and the stories we tell of our lives".

She went on over the following days to talk more about post-structuralist ideas, and narrative therapy. White's ideas on the role of the counsellor as being de-centred and influential (White and Epston 1990; White 1985) and how the goal of therapy was not for the person to go deeper within themselves to grow and actualise, but to move outwards developing having "thicker richer descriptions of their life experiences" (White 2001:26). I tried out some of these ideas in my practice moving from trying to be an expert and understand what was going on for people, to seeing them as the expert in their lives and my role as that of a co-researcher (Epston 2004) who stood alongside encouraging these thicker richer descriptions. I began to understand more about the relational nature of stories, and the importance of the audience within the story telling. Frank (1995) notes that stories are always told *to* someone "whether that other person is immediately present or not" (Frank 1995:3) and the person they are told to, the audience, will influence and inform how the story is told. People responded to these ideas. I did not lose the other knowledge that I had gained over the years, and sometimes would ask people consulting me whether using a particular theory or way of thinking as a metaphor helped them to understand what was going on in their lives.

---

[1] Dr Jane Speedy is a Reader in Qualitative Inquiry at the University of Bristol.

Suddenly even really serious life threatening situations such as suicidal thoughts could be worked with in creative ways. If these suicidal thoughts were seen just as one of the stories about someone's life, rather than the only thing about them, then this implied there might be other stories the person could tell. If identity was socially constructed through story then a person may be able to "re-author" (White 1995) their lives. Instead of seeing the person as the problem, suicidal thoughts could be externalised[2] and their relationship with the person explored. This felt very different from locating the suicidal thoughts inside the person. There is a profound difference from a person saying "I am suicidal" to "I am a person who has a relationship with suicidal thoughts, feelings and behaviours". Within the latter position the person has the freedom to explore what it means to be "in relationship" with these thoughts feelings and behaviours and therefore has the opportunity to change that relationship. O'Neill states, "creating settings which it is accepted that some people are subject to suicidal thoughts and where there is a possibility of actually talking about what these thoughts are on about, what their effects are, and where it is possible to ask questions about these thoughts was seen by the co-researchers as very useful" (O'Neill 2004:40).

It was around this time that I first met Alex. Emailing him following our first counselling session[3] I asked him what he thought was important for us to focus on in our work together. This was his first email to me:

Email from: alex
sent: 6th Feb 2000

Hi lol,
Have been thinking about what you asked me. I think what I need is a better story to live in! This one is crap and I don't like any of the characters or the plot. Have you got a magic wand? Ha ha....
Catch you later Alex

---

[2] Externalising is a practice used by narrative therapists that separates the person from the problem for a good example of this see White (1985)
[3] It is common practice for narrative therapists to write to the people who consult them during the course of their work to re-cap on what they have noticed or has come to their attention following the consultation. For a good example of this practice see Hutton (2008)

Introducing narrative therapy practices to my counselling practice has been something that has transformed my work, and that of the people consulting me. Many have had, over the years, encounter after encounter with the mental health services and medical practitioners who have reduced them to symptoms and diagnosis, and suicidal thoughts are often thought of as wrong thinking. Angela comments, "suicidal thoughts like to tell me that I'm bad and that I don't fit in society" (O'Neill 2004:41). Using a narrative approach that allows people to stand outside other people's assumptions and diagnosis enables a discussion about how the level of distress experienced could, "stand as a testament to what is cherished, believed in and hoped for by a person" (White 2003:35).

I was rather sceptical about my ability to conduct research, but as this was a requirement of a master's degree I wanted to find a methodology that was congruent with these narrative therapy/counselling practices, and that considered reality as socially constructed.

I waded through literature relating to social science research methodologies and soon discovered narrative inquiry, and noticed how it had been used by social science researchers to explore the particularities of lived experience. I also discovered that it was a wide overarching term that meant different things to different people. Narrative researchers came from a wide range of backgrounds "marrying science and the humanities, integrating systematic study of phenomena with literary deconstruction of texts and hermeneutic analyses of meaning" (Josselson, Lieblich, and McAdams 2003:5). It ranged from writers such as Williams (1984) and McAdams (1993) who position their research against what Speedy describes as "archetypal stories or plots" (Speedy 2007:6) others such as Etherington (2000) Reissman (2008; 2002) McLeod (2006) and Speedy (2005) who explored individual stories as significant episodes which illuminated the particular experiences of a person or persons in a particular time scale. Speedy says about her own writing, "this book is not about *whole* life experiences, but about the moments and turning points in people's lives that they struggle to make sense of their lives" (Speedy 2007:6).

There were those such as Mc Adams (1993) who considered collecting narratives of peoples lives and then looking for an underlying "truth" in order to generate theory. There were others such as Hooks (1994) , Brown, Gollop et al (1997) and Langellier (2001) who used the narratives to give voice to marginalised groups. Some like Richardson presented poetic representations of conversation Richardson (2000; 1990; 2000). Others such as Greenspan (2003) presented the narratives in prose.

I felt somewhat lost within this myriad of ideas. I was cognitively aware that any narratives I produced within a research process might socially construct both my own and my participants' sense of identity, and therefore I sought a process that would not analyse the narratives for themes and emerging theory, I would not be searching for an intrinsic truth, but would see the narratives as the analysis. I also noticed that narrative therapists often referred to their work as "co-research" (White and Epston 1990; Epston 2004). However, although I ascribed to these views, for some reason I still expected that the research process would be separate from the therapeutic encounter, and had not anticipated that using a narrative research methodology would change the therapeutic equilibrium.

I suppose I was naïve, and trying hard to adhere to ethical principles that governed counselling research. These emphasised the different purposes of research and counselling. I tried hard to separate the "researcher me" from the "counsellor me". The idea was to create a narrative which would give the reader a glimpse of the experience of having conversations about suicide and I expected that this would be a sort of opening of a window on my therapeutic practice for others to have a look in.

What I discovered however, was that as I started to write with Alex, we were indeed opening up a window on these experiences, but, as fast as we were writing about our experiences, and presenting them on the page we were also writing a new narrative (via our emails) over the top of them. We were re-constructing our relationship, our sense of who we were. Alex was again renegotiating his relationships with suicidal thoughts and was experiencing the research as an extension of the therapeutic process (Etherington 2001).

Fear consumed me. Surely the research and the researcher were supposed to be different, and separate from the counselling, they had different purposes? My academic supervisor however seemed unsurprised and unconcerned giving me further reading from researchers including Hart and Crawford-Wright (1999), Etherington (2000; 2001) and Oritz (2001) exploring the nature of narrative research and its' links with counselling. Alex told me very firmly, "for God sake Sue get a grip"[4]. He had expected the research process to be therapeutic, and this was one of the reasons he wanted to be involved.

I was just so lost in theory and thinking about ethical responsibility that I was a few steps behind. I was, I realised, working on the border between narrative therapy and narrative research, and felt that by using the principles of narrative therapy and being ethically mindful (Bond 2000) rather than only trying to apply guidelines relating to informed consent and the participants rights relating to the outcomes of the study I could renegotiate and engage with boundaries and responsibilities in a new way, and then felt less wobbly and more able to continue.

Speedy speaks of a similar journey from a different direction where she uses narrative practices within her research and then moves these influences into her counselling practice:

> "when it seemed to me that my research interviews were more effective and more therapeutic than my counselling sessions, these ideas began to seep into my therapeutic practice as well" (Speedy 2007:10).

Reflexivity in counselling research

Whatever kind of counselling or research we undertake we bring our "self" with us. Even a quantitative research project that does not specifically refer to the researcher's personal thoughts, feelings and behaviours, which has been approached with a view that subjectivity is "a contaminant" (Etherington 2004:25) will still (even if covertly) be influenced by who the researchers are, what they are interested in, the kind of research questions they are asking and how they analyse and report data collected.

As counsellors we are taught (whatever theoretical model we follow) to be aware of our own responses, our thoughts feelings, and behaviours in response to our clients, the people around us, and to the cultural and social settings we live and practice. Etherington states "to be reflexive we need to be *aware* of our personal responses and to be able to make choices about how to use them" (Etherington 2004:19). How we use this awareness will be dependent on how we see these being relevant to the

---

[4] see emails included at the end of chapter five.7

therapeutic or research process. For example, if I consider that there is an intrinsic truth about something or someone with whom I am conducting a therapeutic or research relationship I may choose to withhold my own personal thoughts feelings and behaviours in order that they have space to explore their own inner world and find meanings (Jacobs 1998). If however I am working from the perspective of seeing reality as socially constructed then I may use my own thoughts feelings and behaviours to create a relationship with others that enables us together to re-define who we are (White 2001).

There seems to be a stark difference between emphasis on individual experience and community experience. Speedy speaks of the modern developments in modern western culture that have "disguised the social and historical roots of what are considered to be 'personal' concerns" (Speedy 2007:7), and when I consider my work with counselling clients over the years I can see how the focus on individuality has at times located the "problem" firmly within the individual, sometimes these "problems" have been more concerned with the person's relationship with their community and social politics such as living with poverty, medical ideas on mental health and disability, social class, and unemployment to name but a few.

Bird speaks of the "relational" practice of conversation (Bird 2000, 2004), and as a narrative practitioner it is the relational aspect of the therapeutic encounters that interested me and that was the focus of my research. What was happening in the therapeutic relationship when we had conversations about suicide? What was happening in the research relationship when we had conversations about the conversations?

I have tried therefore to be reflexive, that is transparent about my own processes and how they have changed and developed as the process has moved on, but even in their final form they are not seen as final and fixed. As they are published and read by you the reader they are again changed. As Etherington comments of her own writing,

"This book is about a process of becoming-it implies movement, agency and continuity, rather than a striving to reach a state at which we have 'become'. It is based upon the notion that we are constantly changing and developing our identities, and that they are never fixed." (Etherington 2004:15).

This is also how I view this publication, it is a process of becoming, our identities never fixed.

The interface between counselling and research

As stated earlier this research project has hovered between the borders of narrative therapy and narrative research practices, and I wanted here to tease out some of the similarities and differences and explore the writings of others who inhabit these borderlands and cross the boundaries between counselling and research. Speedy comments of this journeying:

> "This is something of an open invitation towards trouble. If it doesn't invoke trouble with the gods and goddesses of social science research, it may stir up trouble among the gatekeepers of professional therapeutic endeavour" (Speedy 2007:102).

Why do it then? Well I suppose I knew from my own, and also from colleagues experiences, that having conversations about suicide was one of the most challenging things we encountered within our professional lives. To find a way of exploring what was making it so challenging seemed really important. I was also aware that people who talk about suicide are often at the margins of society and often silenced. They are talked about in terms of statistics, risk, and prevention strategies. I wanted to use research as a way of redressing the balance and giving voice to Alex and others like him who have used suicide as a way of coping with extreme emotional pain.

It has always been important that my work as a counsellor is informed by an internalised "way of being" with people and how I see them able to make changes in their lives rather than an activity where I use a toolbox of counselling skills that can be learnt, and then applied, only when in a counselling context. This means that when entering a research setting, although I can learn new research skills, my internalised "way of being" will affect how I relate to people, and will follow me into any research relationships. If I am going to undertake research, especially if it is with someone who has known me as a counsellor, there is bound to be some kind of overlap and dual relationship. It seems more ethical to be transparent about the overlap than to pretend it does not exist. As Bond states,

> "The dual relationship created by practitioners undertaking research on their own counselling or psychotherapeutic service is very likely to affect,

either positively or negatively, both the therapy and the research" (Bond 2004:6).

If the dual relationship (or my way of being) was going to have some kind of effect on my research activities with Alex then it seemed important that this should be a positive effect rather than a negative one.

To give an example of the conflict that a dual relationship may bring let us consider for a moment purpose. The purposes of counselling and research are usually different. Within a counselling relationship the client consults with the counsellor and the focus is on the issues the client sees as important. Within a research relationship the researcher consults with the participant and the focus is usually on the issues that the researcher considers important. Alex had (following the end of our counselling) remained in contact via email-he thought of me he says like "a phone a friend". I had assumed that my explanation of the differences between our counselling relationship and the proposed research relationship clearly illuminated the differences, but as I was soon to learn; because of my way of being, the felt reality for him was that this "research" was merely therapy in a different format.

I was interested however that within narrative therapy practices the purposes of therapy and research are less clearly differentiated. Often clients are referred to as "co-researchers" (Epston 2004; Hutton 2008) and the purpose is often seen as one of standing alongside the client to research their life experiences. Co-researchers are often encouraged to link their lives with others with similar experiences such that the therapy is not something just located in the counselling room, but within wider communities.

By overtly placing this project with Alex in the border land between narrative therapy and narrative research practices, and ensuring that Alex's purposes for undertaking the research project have been met, meant that I could bridge some of the gaps created by the dual relationship of counsellor and researcher. It seemed to be the most respectful way of undertaking research that would be congruent with my way of working therapeutically. I was aware however that this kind of project would be ethically challenging.

Narrative ethics when writing other peoples stories

Moving between the borders of counselling into research appeared to require paying special attention to both the ethical principles underpinning counselling and counselling research practices. There is also, as discussed earlier the problem of conducting narrative research where people are telling intimate stories of their life within a context where there is a dual relationship or an existing relationship outside the context of the research. Ellis states,

> "relational ethics requires researchers to act from our hearts and minds, acknowledge our interpersonal bonds to others and take responsibility for actions and their consequences" (Ellis 2007:3).

Bond writing on the question of counselling and psychotherapy research uses the ethical principle of trust and trustworthiness between the researcher and the researched both in terms of the practicalities of safeguarding data, and also in terms of the relationship (Bond 2004, 2000). Trust seems imperative and more than just an academic exercise and the trust invested in me as a counsellor must run through into any research relationship. From the client's perspective although my role is different and I have a different purpose for talking with them, their purpose for talking to me may be influenced by our earlier relationship, and they may trust me because of my role as a counsellor, not necessarily comprehending how different the research process may be. I have the skills as a counsellor to elicit stories, I could use these to engage people in conversations that perhaps they would prefer to keep private rather than be the material of a research project.

My way of engaging with these dilemmas is through reflexivity and I try to be as transparent as possible with regard to both my motives and actions relating to research. As Etherington points out "the link between reflexivity and ethical research seems to rest on transparency" (Etherington 2007:604). How can a research participant trust me to tell their stories within a narrative account if I am not transparent about the way in which I am going to use their stories? The participants need to understand the context as well as the content.

Speedy says of her narrative research projects, "Whilst I did regularly consult with supervisors during this project, the most rigorous and sustaining support for this work was through constantly consulting with my consultants" (Speedy 2007:52) she goes on to explain this as consulting her research participants who she considers herself "permanently accountable" (ibid:52). Unless we take the time to find out what really matters to the people who are telling us their stories, and how they want to be represented we cannot, I feel engage with the concept of ethical mindfulness (Bond 2000).

White and Epston speak about the narrative therapy practice of regularly checking out with co-researchers that they are "getting it right" (White and Epston 1990). This then re-positions the research participant differently. As Speedy states

"the language of accountability and responsibility towards people consulting us has a very different emphasis and positions researchers very differently from thin descriptions of participants as vulnerable people" (Speedy 2007:52).

There is a move away from seeing the person as someone who is voiceless and that research is "done to", to becoming an expert witness and partner in our research activities.

This consultation and accountability has also to reflect on the way we present someone else's story on the page and the context in which this page is then published to wider audiences.

Clough (2002) uses fictionalised stories to illustrate some of the outcomes where narrative researchers have placed their research outcomes above the needs of the people being researched. In a fictionalised account he tells the story of Lolly who visits him following the publication of research about his younger brother Molly. Clough has presented words spoken by Lolly and his mother in ways that are accurate, and prove his thesis, but that Molly considers deeply disrespectful. Molly is furious stating:

"So this is where it all happens.....where children are killed. Where families are displayed like circus freaks?" (Clough 2002:55-57)

The anger of Lolly and the embarrassment of Clough the researcher are tangible and uncomfortable to those of us who write other people's stories. How do we present narratives in such a way as to allow readers to have an experience of the story teller without being disrespectful?

How to present Alex and my stories was challenging. I wanted his voice to be central to the study, I wanted him to feel empowered rather than "talked about". When I started to listen to the recordings of our conversation and looked at his journal what really struck me was the poetic nature of his words. I had read several texts which used stanza or poetic narrative format Richardson (1992; 2000), Etherington (2000), Speedy (2005). I suggested that we present his words in stanza format as I thought that this would be a good way of using Alex's own words without me having to change the text to make a grammatically correct account. I was concerned that my editing could change the worlds meaning and dilute their power to communicate, and would be open to misinterpretation.

Within this chapter I hope that I have given a flavour of what it is that I mean by narrative research, and how within this project it has been linked with narrative therapy, and how I have tried to engage with the ethical issues relating to conducting a narrative project such as this.

Etherington (2007) gives some guidelines for ethical research in reflexive relationships which over the course of the research project, and indeed within the writing of this book I have come back to over and over again:

> "To remain aware of the potential power imbalance between researcher and participants, especially where there are current or previous boundary issues created by dual relationships, and where there are issues of race, gender age, etc.
>
> To negotiate research decisions transparently with participants, and to balance our own needs with those of participants and agencies involved;
>
> To provide ongoing information as it becomes available, even when that requires the use of appropriate and judicious researcher self-disclosure;
>
> To include in our writing and representations information about research dilemmas that may occur and the means by which they have been resolved" (Etherington 2007:614).

These it seems give a framework to review the balance between our needs as researchers, and our accountability and obligations towards those we are researching.

Ethical mindfulness it would seem is not about a simple one off decision, but must be integrated within the whole of the research process. Within the next chapter following an exploration of the context in which the study is set, I will go on to explore how the risk of suicide further complicates the ethical decision making.

CHAPTER TWO

SUICIDAL THOUGHTS
IN THE COUNSELLING ROOM

The World Health Organisation considers that suicide is the cause of death for some 873,000 people worldwide each year, and within the UK The Office for National Statistics (2009) reports that in 2007 there were an estimated 5,377 suicides in adults aged 15 and over and as many as what are described as "non-fatal acts of self harm" in 400 out of every 100,000 people (Winter et al. 2009). These figures of course do not include the people who think and feel suicidal but have not acted on these thoughts, or those who have not required hospital treatment.

Introduction

It is my intention within this chapter to look more generally at counselling and the suicidal client and to examine some of the literature available in respect of client and counsellor perspectives on suicide, professional responsibilities and accountability, client rights and responsibilities. I shall then return to the specific project with Alex to explore the ethical challenges faced when researching with an ex-counselling client about suicidal thoughts, feelings and behaviours.

I think this is important as it teases out some of the complex professional responsibilities and ethical dilemmas and gives context and a backdrop against which my work with Alex (both the counselling and research) was conducted.

It is worth the reader remembering that my counselling relationship with Alex goes back ten years, and at the time there was little or no information or training in how to work with suicidal clients, and the BACP new ethical framework for counselling and psychotherapy had only just been launched.

The intervention of years has brought the issues of working with suicidal clients very much to the fore of professional debate, and there have been several government led reviews including one commissioned by the National Institute for Health and Clinical Excellence (NICE) for the purpose of developing clinical practice guidelines (2004) which suggested "few specific interventions for people who have self-harmed that have any positive effect" (cited by Winter et al. 2009:5). In 2009 BACP commissioned a systematic review of research specifically looking at using counselling and psychotherapy for the prevention of suicide. Some of the findings from this review and other qualitative studies are discussed within this chapter.

Within my practice, conversation about suicide is frequent, with referral often specific to this issue. Through my role as a supervisor and trainer I am aware that counsellors are still frequently left not knowing "what to do" if a client reports suicidal thoughts. Few training courses incorporate teaching time on how counsellors can deal with the ethical dilemmas arising out of work with the suicidal. A counsellor participant from Reeves and Mintz (2001) study says of her training, "I don't think we did enough on suicide and I don't think that prepared me for working with people who are suicidal" (Reeves and Mintz 2001:174). Many supervisors are still unsure or unclear in their guidance. Some agencies and organisations have specific instructions and guidelines regarding suicide risk, others leave it to the counsellor's own judgment.

Client and counsellor perspectives regarding suicide

Neale, a counsellor attending a recent training session facilitated by me, commented:

> "The biggest problem for me when encountering a suicidal client is that they think they have found some incredibly creative solution in suicide and expect that I will (as I usually do) empathise and stand alongside them, whereas in fact I see it (suicide) as a major problem that I will do anything to stop. Empathy goes out of the window and I go into full scale panic." (included with permission)

Why do people want to kill themselves?

There seems no simple answer to this question, and has been the subject of much research. Studies as early as Serin (1926) Robins, Sainsbury (1955) Murphy et al. (1959) Dorpat and Riley (1960) used data collected relating to successful suicides. This showed a link between suicide and poor mental health, but although the research shows correlation between these factors, it does not show causation. As O'Conner and Sheehy point out, "the vast majority of those with a mental illness do not kill themselves" (O'Connor and Sheehy 2000:31).

Maris (1991) estimated that 15% of those who were clinically depressed would commit suicide and two thirds of all suicides had a depressive illness. Studies by Guze and Robins (1970) estimated the risk of suicide by those affected by severe mood disorders was 19%. Goodwin and Jamison (1990) concluded that 15% of those with a primary diagnosis of depression commit suicide. Other studies such as Baraclough and Pallis (1975) show the contribution of depression when other psychosocial risk factors are present such as living alone, low self esteem, isolation, reduced social support, insomnia. Other risk factors have been shown to be alcoholism (Marttunen et al. 1991) substance abuse (Harris and Baraclough 1997), a diagnosis of schitzophrenia (Roy 1982a, 1982b) or personality disorder (Baraclough 1987). A history of childhood abuse has also been cited as a significant common feature in those who repeatedly attempted suicide (Browne and Finkelhor 1986; Law et al. 1998) and the risk significantly rises following an earlier suicide attempt. Unemployed socially isolated young men are especially at risk. (Appelby and Warner 1993).

But do these studies really give us an understanding of why people say they want to die?

At some stage in our lives most of us will feel, even if we have no intention of acting on these feelings, that life is not really worth living any more, or will think about (even fleetingly) the possibility of our control over whether we live or die. Stubbs on behalf of the Samaritans opens the forward to Heckler's book commenting, "we are *all* potentially suicidal. We all have the ability to kill ourselves. One possibility that we share in common is: life is optional" (Heckler 1994:xi). Most of us have very good reasons to stay alive, so these thoughts often are unspoken stories that never surface.

If, for a moment, we leave the statistical data, and talk to people who have attempted or thought about suicide then we learn that sometimes when the person experiences intolerable psychological pain, the thought of suicide then becomes an ultimate solution where there seem to be no other choices. Chris a research participant in Heckler's research study comments:

> "The pain was up here in my heart, but in the pit of my stomach it felt like everything just dropped out of me, out the bottom. There was just horror. I had these two bottles of sleeping pills: the doctor kept prescribing them, and I kept on not taking them, just saving them. I knew that would be enough. As I was walking upstairs, I felt cold all through my body, but also determined. It felt like it was the only reasonable thing to do" (Heckler 1994:73).

Others it seems use suicidal thoughts and feelings over a long period of time and see them as a way of having the ultimate control over life. Plath writes:

> "Dying is an art, like everything else.
> I do it exceptionally well.
>
> I do it so it feels like hell.
> I do it so it feels real.
> I guess you could say I've a call". (Plath 1981:245)

Her friend Sexton comments of their relationship "We talked of death and this was life to us" (cited in Etkind 1997:49). Sexton like Plath was a poet who wrote profusely about suicide and ended her life in 1974.

Speaking openly about suicide however is not common practice. It is after all is a highly emotive subject which historically and indeed currently is seen as taboo.

The Christian church from the time of the 6th Century outlawed suicide (O'Connor and Sheehy 2000:6). In the UK the criminal status of suicide did not finally end until 1961 (Williams 1997:17). and up until 1870 and the repeal of the common law felony of self-murder, suicide or "self-murder" was seen as an "offence against God, the King and nature" and suicides could be tried posthumously by a coroners court . If convicted all their assets were forfeit to the Crown. Often suicides were refused a Christian burial, and in some Christian communities this is still the case. From a personal perspective these facts were really brought home to me in

2004 when I worked with a Catholic woman whose son had committed suicide. Her parish priest had refused to undertake a burial service and in response she also attempted suicide.

Although attitudes have changed I consider that these historical factors which are part of our society's past do have an effect on current attitudes, and people (professionals included) have very strong beliefs and conflicting moral attitudes towards suicide. A debate in the Times newspaper during November 2004 illustrates this. "Taking your life is a cowardly betrayal that we should never condone" (Hume 2004). "Suicide is not painless, but it can be brave, right and rational" (Parris 2004). Many contemporary psychological perspectives treat suicidal thoughts and actions as "profoundly abnormal" (O'Connor and Sheehy 2000:9).

Health Care professionals who are dedicated to saving life often find those who repeatedly attempt suicide challenging. Pembroke (1996) states, "Health services and workers often recoil from self-harmers, occasionally to the point of medical negligence" (ibid:3). She goes on to talk about people's experiences of being stitched up with no medical anaesthesia. One of her participants comments about a medical practitioners response to her was, "You must see a psychiatrist-if you don't and you come back here again this will all have been a waste of time" (ibid:7).

If you talk about suicide, there is often a value judgment made that this is a kind of wrong thinking and selfish. Brett says of his visit to a GP to request medication:

"The doctor started talking, which I understand she needed to do, but when she found out that I'd attempted suicide she started to put some sort of guilt-trip on me: 'what about your family? Wasn't that a selfish thing to do?" (O'Neill 2004:41)

Jess says:

"When people are judgmental about suicidal thoughts, if people say you're selfish to have them, or if they say things like imagine how other people would feel if you did that, then this gives suicidal thoughts strength" (ibid:42).

The unassuming geeks[1] write of their experiences of being suicidal:

> "You can only die once but you can think about dying as often as you like"
> (Speedy 2007:132)

They go on to talk about suicide prevention:

> "The UK government has a strategy
> So we are running our lives beneath their radar" (ibid:132)

and:

> "We are vital statistics. A 'worrying' trend". (ibid:133)

People are often afraid to talk about their suicidal thoughts and feelings to health care professionals because they are afraid of the response. As Phillip, one of Pembroke's (1996) participants, says:

> "The greatest condemnation of psychiatry is that some of us would rather be on the brink of destruction than accept what they offer" (Pembroke 1996:3)

Counsellors are human too, although we try always to espouse non-judgmental positive regard (Rogers 1961) we are not only affected by the historical grand narratives surrounding suicide, and our own prejudices and feelings about suicide, but also we recognise that as professionals we have certain responsibilities, and sometimes feel that, "if I don't do the right thing this person may end up dead. The sense of hopelessness that comes with suicide infects me like a cold virus!" (Beth a counsellor on a training course. Included with permission). As O'Neale comments, "when someone walks in the door of our office and starts to talk about suicide and suicidal thoughts, our sense of hopelessness has the potential to render us as workers either impotent or panic ridden" (O'Neill 2004:40).

Sometimes our own personal views come into conflict with our professional training, and the organisational views of our employers. One of Reeves and Mintz (2001) research participants states,

---

[1] This is a group of young men connected by suicide who write collectively. The group was originally facilitated by Jane Speedy. You can read more about them and collective biography within Speedy (2007).

"just by knowing that I need my job and that if I don't abide by them I am likely to be looked at very closely for using my personal view as opposed to what their wishes are" (ibid:49).

Suicide as Pritchard (1995) points out is often seen as the ultimate rejection. As counsellors we can feel that our reputation, and skill as a counsellor, is being questioned. As Neale a counsellor on a training course said to me:

"I was obviously a crap counsellor, the person in front of me preferred the idea of dying to having further counselling sessions to sort out their problems" (included with permission).

Within the counselling professions caring for the suicidal can be seen as "totally inappropriate" (Collins 1988:115) or unworkable. Brian Thorne writes, "I believe that my own inner "wobbliness" and my sense of responsibility for the other person made it virtually impossible for me to engage with suicidal clients at a level where a real meeting could take place" (Thorne 1991:86), or that as Morgan (1993) states, "we have a responsibility to encourage the wish to live" (cited by Williams 1997:1).Winter Bradshaw et al. comment within their review,

"one of the most prominent aspects identified in this synthesis was the nature of suicide and self-harm and the connotations associated with this behaviour that can impact on effective therapy" (Winter et al. 2009:53).

Professional responsibilities and accountability

As counsellors our practices are governed firstly by the laws of the land, secondly through our adherence to ethical guidelines and codes of practice set out by the professional bodies to which we belong and thirdly to our own personal views of ethics and morality. It is not my intention here to discuss in depth the law and its relationship with counselling. Readers interested can find relevant information within the texts of Bond (2000) and Jenkins (2002). Neither can I comment on personal ethics and morality, except from a purely personal perspective, but what I intend to explore is how these factors may influence how counsellors interpret the ethical codes set out by the professional bodies that govern counselling and psychotherapy.

Although there are several UK professional counselling and psychotherapy bodies with codes of ethics for practice, the largest whose ethical framework I adhere to, and that is discussed belongs to the BACP which, rather than a list of "do's and don'ts" encourage what Bond (2000) describes as ethical mindfulness .

Counsellors are encouraged to engage with their practice in accordance with ethical values, principles, and personal moral qualities rather than a list of rules[2]. The framework tries to give assistance to practitioners faced with ethical dilemmas (such as suicidal clients). They state:

> "These ethics are intended to be of assistance in such circumstances by directing attention to the variety of ethical factors that may need to be taken into consideration and to alternative ways of approaching ethics that may prove more useful" (BACP 2009:4).

So let us consider for a moment what some of these ethical challenges may be:

Probably the most challenging ethical issue that occurs when working with a suicidal client is whether as a counsellor we take "seeking to protect life" as a supreme ethical cornerstone for our work, or whether we respect client autonomy, even if this means that the client may choose to die?

Do we empathise, explore the suicidal thoughts with our clients and take no action, or do we need (or want) to alert others, most usually the client's GP, or other medical practitioner, of the perceived danger?

Some clients of course may wish, or agree to the counsellor contacting a medical professional, other clients demand the right to confidentiality. Then as Bond comments, "the counsellor is faced with a choice between respecting the client's autonomy or seeking to preserve life, either because this is considered to be a fundamental ethical principle or because it is thought to be in the client's best interest" (Bond 2000:96). Some agencies have clear protocols and guidelines which help the counsellor make decisions in this kind of situations, others do not.

The dilemma is made more complex because if someone expresses suicidal thoughts, feelings and behaviours this does not mean that their rights to confidentiality and autonomy are forfeit. Under the Mental Health Act 1983 there is no provision for compulsory assessment or treatment just because someone is suicidal. Shneidman points out, "All persons who

---

[2] For a full description of the ethical framework go to www.bacp.org.uk

commit suicide–100 per cent of them–are perturbed, but they are not necessarily clinically depressed (or schizophrenic or alcoholic or addicted or psychiatrically ill)". (Shneidman 1993). Bond goes on to say that English law is strongly weighted in favour of respecting individual autonomy (Bond 2000:100). If the counsellor however has "reasonable grounds for believing that the client is seriously at risk of committing suicide and is suffering from a treatable mental disorder, e.g. depression, schizophrenia" (ibid: 103) then they may be able to argue justification for breaching confidentiality in order for medical professionals to assess whether the person should be compelled to receive compulsory treatment under the Mental Health Act.

Jenkins gives a small case study to illustrate this point. The client rejects the counsellor's request to contact her GP because she will require medical references and reports in order to pursue her career. The counsellor does contact her GP with the consequence that the client's future career is adversely affected. "The client sues for breach of confidence and substantial damages for loss of earnings" (Jenkins 2002:127).

Even if the counsellor gets permission to contact a GP or mental health professional and the agency (or supervisor) is content for the counsellor to continue working with the client, there is still the matter of how a counsellor can manage their own thoughts and feelings relating to suicide and the possibility of their client dying. Working with suicidal clients has been cited as one of the highest stressors for counsellors (Russel 1989; Menninger 1991). Richards conducted a study into the impact upon therapy and the therapist when working with suicidal clients. One of her counsellor participants states, "I experienced something of his desperation and feelings of helplessness and hopelessness" (Richards 2000:334). She concludes. "The present study has demonstrated how therapeutic work with patients who tend to act out their distress in self-destructive ways is demanding in the extreme" (Richards 2000:336). This is echoed within Winter, Bradshaw et al. review (2009) where they summarise, "Difficulties in treating the suicidal client were indicated by the therapists' and counsellors feelings of ambience" (ibid:53).

So I suppose the question for me is, if suicidal clients prove so challenging to work with, why do we do it?

There are of course some, as discussed earlier in this chapter, who say that we should not. Several of the therapists interviewed by Richards (2000) believed that it would be preferable to see such people within an institutional setting rather than private practice, because within an institutional setting they could be monitored and prohibited from harming themselves.

Certainly counsellors need to be well supported if they are going to undertake this kind of work, and able to negotiate all of the ethical challenges faced.

The reason I undertake this work is that the people who consult me tell me they find it helpful, and they usually go on to live full lives. For me, if someone is "talking" about suicide it means there may be possibilities also for "talking" about life (I'm a great believer in life!) and alternative stories for the future. If someone was certain that suicide was the only way forward, they would not be talking, but acting. As you read the narrative account of my work with Alex, you will be able to make your own judgements as to whether it was worthwhile. These days I only work with suicidal clients in consultation with my supervisor, and if the person is happy for me to work in conjunction with their GP or mental health team. It is not a decision I take lightly, and one of my requirements is that they are open to exploring alternatives to suicide.

Client rights and responsibilities

So do our client's have any rights and responsibilities? Or is counselling even helpful? Jess one of O'Neill's participant's talks of her experiences of therapy:

> "Not being alone in it is the biggest thing for me. Being isolated is the worst because then no other logic can come in and I become trapped. It's when I am alone that suicidal thoughts and depression and anxiety and all those kinds of forces can take over a lot more" (O'Neill 2004:42).

In later chapters you will hear what Alex felt was helpful about counselling and what was not. My current practices have been informed by my work (both counselling and research) with Alex and others. They are, I consider, the experts in their lives and give us guidelines for our practice as counsellors.

From the client's perspective, I consider that all our clients have the right to expect that any counsellor they work with respects them no matter what their thoughts feelings and behaviours might be. This includes respecting their right to autonomy but in a way that also holds respect and concern for their safety.

Pembroke based on her research with young people who self harm makes a list of suggestions for counsellors which seem helpful including:

"Abandon your assumptions
Change Your priorities from diagnosis and treatment to:
   a)   listen
   b)   seek out the person's own knowledge
   c)   act on that information
   d)   take the person seriously" (Pembroke 1996:56)

Whilst I recognise that many client's do not enter counselling specifically to talk about their suicidal thoughts and feelings, if I were a client who did wish to have these kind of conversations, I would want to know whether the counsellor had any kind of framework or guidelines for how these conversations might happen, whether they would need to speak with my GP or mental health practitioner, and what the limits of confidentiality may be, and whether they had any experience of working with these kind of issues, and I would need above all to feel safe, listened to and in control of my destiny.

Some suggestion has been made that suicidal clients should be asked to sign a "no suicide" contract whilst engaging with counselling, but there is little to suggest that this is of benefit to either the counsellor or the client (Winter, Bradshaw et al. 2009).

To summarise: research review (Winter et al. 2009) concludes that there is strong evidence of the effectiveness of psychotherapy and counselling in preventing suicide, and certainly the other literature examined here also echo's this. The reviewers also noted from their analysis that,

"difficulties in treating the suicidal client were indicated by the therapists' and counsellors' feelings of ambivalence in the process studies. These feelings may override aspects such as the therapist's level of competence" (ibid:53).

What does not seem to have been addressed is how we as counsellors can become less ambivalent in our work with suicidal clients. It is also noted within the review that,

"therapists who show respect, understanding, validation of feelings and a non-judgmental attitude are viewed most positively by clients at risk from suicide" (ibid:53).

Perhaps naively I thought that these qualities were ones that were of paramount importance to all the clients we work with whether suicidal or not!

One of Spandler's research participants talks about the reasons why psychotherapy is difficult for her. She states:

"Some people get the impression that if I talk about some of these things that I'm going to do something like that afterwards. A psychotherapist wouldn't accept me because of what I might have done afterwards, that's why they wouldn't accept me, because of my behaviour and they thought it might make me worse. I think that's wrong" (Spandler 2003:82).

If this is the attitudes of psychotherapists (and counsellors) for whatever reason, then I agree with her. It does indeed seem wrong and something that as a profession we have to address.

Ethics and dilemmas when researching with suicidal clients

Having explored some of the ethical dilemmas of undertaking counselling with suicidal clients, and also the ethical challenges of researching with counselling clients, and writing other people's stories within narrative research now I want to return to the specifically to my research project with Alex and to think about whether researching specifically with a client who had been suicidal posed any further ethical dilemmas.

I was a very new researcher, and as stated previously my greatest fear was that in undertaking this project with Alex and compiling narratives about his thoughts, feelings and behaviours about suicide this would take him back to a place where he again felt suicidal.

As Josselson (1996) states, "Do you really feel like interfering in his or her life? Will you be able to live with the consequences of this encounter or intervention? Is it justified from the interviewees own perspective" (Josselson 1996:9). It also felt a very different position to ask Alex for help as opposed to him asking me. The role reversal changed the dynamics. With this in mind, and in retrospect I suspect to satisfy any perspective examiner, I produced a list of questions to discuss with both Alex and my supervisor prior to the project that I hoped would enable me to engage with the ethical challenges.

The questions were:

1. Would Alex be re-immersed into feelings of despair and thoughts of suicidal fantasy
2. Would he feel "shamed" or distressed in any way by the conversations? Lee points out that there are areas of personal experience, which are "emotionally charged" (Lee 1993:6) which could result in the interviewee becoming highly uncomfortable and stressed.
3. Would he have enough support systems? Being a "researcher" would be different from my "counselling" role. Etherington refers to this dilemma whilst researching with ex-clients stating that it "may not be possible to revert to the therapist role" (Etherington 2001:8).
4. Could Alex say "no". Because of the power dynamic between counsellor and client, the client or even an ex-client may feel they have no option but to say "yes", and there was also the question of my power to present the research in which I think is appropriate. As Etherington points out "we have power in the way we choose to analyse or interpret the meaning of data we collect and in our choice of audience for whom we write or present our research findings" (Etherington 2000:263).
5. How could Alex's privacy be maintained? I wanted to ensure that what I wrote did not compromise Alex's request for anonymity.

At the time I felt very diligent and responsible. Alex responded to my questions (as you will see in later chapters) with a degree of amusement and irritation. He was able and wanted to take responsibility for his participation, my "wobbliness" and thinking of him as vulnerable irritated him. He wanted me to see him as autonomous and able to make his own decisions about his involvement and engagement with suicidal thoughts and feelings. My wobbliness as well as irritating him also reassured him that I was taking his safety seriously which he felt was a good thing.

In retrospect I suspect that my wobbliness was also about whether I wanted to relive and reveal to other professionals my own vulnerabilities when undertaking this work. It was ok for Alex and my counselling supervisor to know how I felt as I worked with him, but did I want other counsellors, and even academics to judge either of us?

Whereas Alex could remain anonymous, I could not, the research project would be written in my name.

CHAPTER THREE

INTRODUCING ALEX

Introduction

The preceding chapters have tried to set the scene in respect of my work with Alex, and they have predominately been my views and reflections on literature and how I have chosen to make sense of the world I live and work in. Within this chapter the focus moves to Alex and introduces him, firstly from his own perspective and then together we explore what is the central theme for the chapter: power, knowledge and control, and how these affected our work together (both the counselling and research). Then there is an exploration of how narrative practices can be used to negotiate different kinds of power and knowledge and to explore the particularities of lived experience.

Email
from: Alex4research
Sent: 06Dec 2009 02:32

Hello out there,
I'm Alex. Well Alex isn't my real name, or all of me. It is the name I am for these stories, and Alex is part of me, and always will be, he's the bit of me that had to start letting go of the idea of dying and turn towards living. He had a very tough journey, and so did my family and Sue!

Sue asked me what I'd like her to say to introduce myself-well where do I start?

I guess rather than start at the beginning I'll start where I am now and why you're reading about my life at a time when it felt like wading through shit would be an easy option.

I now work as a counsellor for a substance misuse team. I completed my counselling studies at what used to be called the "polly" but now has been "university-fied". I think I'm ok at the job, although lots of the clients find it hard to even turn up for sessions, let alone want to change, they often tell me they'd prefer to be dead, it's hard then not to preach at them! I had a lot of practice as a client, and know all the tricks of the trade and that has helped I think!

I'm married and have got a little kid of my own now. Life has it's ups and downs, but I'm really glad that I'm here to enjoy it.

I think what really helped Alex most was meeting someone who didn't judge him or tell him that he had "wrong thinking". All the shrinks always tried to make me feel guilty about trying to end my life. They often asked "why are you doing this" but not with an attitude of trying to understand, only with an attitude of "this has got to stop". And the more they tried to make me stop, the more the thoughts took hold and the more I wanted to die.

When Sue asked me if I would be interested in doing some research with her I said yes. I wanted to know what it was about meeting with her that had helped. I expected that she would tidy all my talking and spelling up and write some learned paper that experts would nod their heads to and criticise.

She is always one to buck the system though and come up with the unexpected.

I will never forget opening the first poem she sent me, it took my breath away and the kid who had been firmly shut in a dark cupboard for a year or two emerged. I wasn't frightened of him any more, I remember crying, but not the kind of tears that made me want to die, the kind of tears that were about liberating him from somewhere he had got stuck.

I suppose what I realise looking back was that thinking about suicide was the think that kept me alive. When everything is out of your control sometimes the only thing you do have control over is whether you keep breathing.
I think it is really important that counsellors take the risk of working with people like Alex, but I know that it is a tough call and that's why I'm really glad to still be talking with Sue, and that our stories are going to be turned into a book.

Suicidal thoughts thrive on secrecy. Out in the open they can be talked about alongside alternative thoughts and solutions.

Sexual abuse also thrives on secrecy; this was why that kid thought the only way out was to stop breathing. Sexual abuse is about power and control, and as a small boy he had neither of those. He is ok now though, he has Alex and me to protect him.

Hope my ramblings have added something!
Alex

A counsellor's first impression

Alex was 35 when I first met him. I was working as a counsellor in private practice, and often received referrals from local GP's and mental health teams to work specifically with people who self-harmed or had attempted suicide. I also ran an "in house" counselling service for a local MIND group.

I contacted Alex's GP[1] following my first meeting with him, and the GP replied:

"...this patient makes almost daily appointments to see one of us, and has made to our knowledge 10 suicide attempts which required hospitalization over the last 2 years. He frequently self-harms and refuses medication. He has a history of alcohol and drug misuse. He has been assessed by (name of psychiatrist) who has stated that he does not have a diagnosable mental health disorder and he has been subsequently discharged as no suitable treatment has been identified".

The words of the letter made me nervous, in a way that meeting Alex had not. Would I be able to live up to the GP's expectation I wondered? What were Alex's expectations of the counselling?

This was the starting point of a lengthy counselling relationship where gradually our expectations of each other were negotiated and I had little or no further contact with the GP in question. We met over a two year period for a total of 69 sessions at a local community centre.

Following the end of our counselling relationship Alex kept in contact with the occasional email. He agreed soon after the ending of the counselling to undertake a small joint project with me where we produced a small collaborative study reviewing our counselling relationship, this was submitted as part of my MSc coursework. When I contacted him

---

[1] It is my normal practice to ask the client for permission to write to their GP if I consider there to be a risk of suicide or self harm.

regarding the possibility of undertaking a slightly larger project which would culminate in a dissertation he was very enthusiastic. He had just started counselling training and wanted to explore his experiences for his own personal development.

We decided that the focus of our research together was going to be specifically related to the conversations we had about suicide. We decided not to focus on the many other conversations we had on the various other stories which make up Alex's life.

Power, control and knowledge are central to this chapter. Alex has already mentioned "control" in respect of suicidal thoughts in his introduction so I intend now to explore what could be meant by these words.

Power, control, and knowledge

I have become interested in Foucault's (Foucault 1984, 1980) descriptions of traditional power and modern power. Traditional power being seen as something which "establishes social control through a system of institutionalised moral judgement that is exercised by the appointed representatives of the state" (White 2002:44) and modern power which establishes social control through "a system of normalising judgement that is exercised by people in the evaluation of their own and each others lives" (ibid:44).

Foucault considered knowledge and power to be inseparable, "we are subjected to the production of truth through power and we cannot exercise power except through the production of truth" (Foucault 1980:93). I consider that perhaps this should be expanded to also include control. For example within academia certain types of knowledge are considered to be more valuable than others. Expert written texts are often valued more than personal experience and local knowledge. Those who have the "valued" knowledge have power to construct judgment systems (such as degree courses) so that individuals can prove they have the relevant knowledge. The academic institutions therefore have control over how and what we learn, and the way in which many professions emerge. Counselling is no exception, over the last two decades with a move towards government registration of practitioners there has been within training courses a move away from the "doing" of the counselling and the practical skills required, to the theorising and writing about how it should be done. Professional bodies have emerged which have moved the emphasis from client centred practices (Rogers 1978) to evidence led practice (the evidence collected and collated by expert academics) and the power over who practices as a counsellor and how they practice comes from these professional bodies rather than what the people who access the services. Foucault (1980) refers to this as a descending analysis of power which as White and Epston (1990) point out,

> "include techniques for the organization and arrangement of persons in space in ways that allowed for the greatest efficiency and economy; those for the registrations and classifications of persons and for the ascription of identity to these groups; techniques for the isolation of persons and for the effective means of observation (surveillance) and evaluation" (White and Epston 1990:24).

These practices dominate our health services, including mental health services, and how they approach people with diagnosis and treatment regimes.

When I first met Alex what struck me most about him was that his experience of having opportunity to speak about his suicidal thoughts, feelings and behaviours was very limited. His needs and views were not respected, and he was powerless.

Alex seemed to me to be trapped by both modern and traditional power structures of institutionalized moral judgement of the mental health professionals who told him that, "suicide is not an acceptable behaviour" and by powerful social attitudes that consider suicidal thoughts "wrong thinking". These attitudes can be seen clearly within national initiatives to reduce suicide rates such as the publication of the National Suicide Prevention Strategy for England (Dept Health 2002). The implication for counselling is that, "suicide prevention and reduction should be a priority for all therapists" (Reeves and Seber 2004:45). This implies that suicide is indeed "wrong thinking".

When Foucault (1984; 1980) talks about modern power he sees this as influenced by the traditional power sources, but is a power that ascends rather than descends. It establishes control through the society in which people live, and brings a system of normalising judgements made by those societies, which people strive to aspire to. Within the UK I consider these include judgements that we should:

- have a right to happiness
- pursue self-improvement in the form of education, occupation and social standing
- pursue wealth
- pursue a relationship with a significant other (usually of the opposite sex)
- be able bodied and fit
- strive for professionalization
- that here is a "right way" to conduct a therapeutic relationship

These judgments may differ of course depending on the society or communities a person is involved with and could also be influenced by media coverage or government propaganda.

White (1999; 2007) explores the whole question of personal failure in light of the mechanisms of traditional and modern power, and how certain groups of people can feel marginalised and disempowered.

Those who see suicidal thoughts and behaviours as legitimate responses to their life experiences are marginalised voices who can easily be lost within the "ought's" and "should's" of both hierarchical power systems and socially normalising judgments of communities and society. Unless there is a move to enable these marginalised voices to be heard this inequality will exist unchecked.

White considers that there is "a relationship between the intensity of a persons experience of failure and the distance they have assigned themselves and been assigned by others from the cherished and socially constructed norms" (White 2003:46) for what it means to be a person of worth in our culture.

For Alex personal failure was about not maintaining a relationship he cherished, for being abused, and for "failing as a suicide". For me personal failure was about my own failure to live up to what I considered were the "norms" of counselling. Within my counselling relationship with Alex there was a conflict between my methodology; that considered Alex to be the expert in his life, and what the counselling "norms" expected of counsellors; which at the time did not include working with the suicidal.

As discussed in previous chapters respecting and trusting Alex's right to autonomy was of paramount importance, and as you read the narratives emerging from our counselling sessions you will notice the way in which both traditional and modern power systems influenced our work together. Using a counselling methodology which respected Alex's autonomy was vital to our navigation of these power systems as this empowered, rather than disempowered, Alex to take control of his life. Also by moving him from someone who was "vulnerable" and had to be taken care of and treated, to a position of being a co-researcher, someone I was accountable to, changed the power dynamic between us, and this when transferred into the research relationship narrowed the gap between the researcher and the researched and gave Alex some control over the research process.

I met with Alex recently to discuss the publication of this book, and asked him how (or if) he thought power, knowledge and control had anything to do with our work together.

Conversations with Alex December 2009

Sue: I've been trying to write something in the book about power, control and knowledge
How do you.
or do you see them as having anything to do with our work together?

Alex: Yes
Power and control
always , not sure about knowledge..
but power and control have everything to do with it.

As a little kid,
the gang who used to rape me
    and all the other stuff
they did it because they could.
It made them feel powerful
in control.
They could do it
and **I had no power** and **no control to stop** it.
I suppose that's where knowledge comes in too
They knew I had no-one that I could talk to
No-one on my side.

They knew my mum wouldn't ask
I knew they were right
and **I didn't know what to do**

I got some control
and in my mind some control meant power
I got it when I thought about dying.

I could choose whether to live or not
The ultimate control was mine.

He was quite a bright kid really
up against huge odds.

Sue: Yes. You know that I've always been a major supporter of him!
What about later?
What about later in life
Did power and control mean something then?

Alex: Yes
Again,
everything.

You know the psychy hut[2]
Everything there is about power and control and knowledge.
They know best.
Your thinking is wrong.
They take all the control.
There is nothing left then...
of you as a person
just emptiness.
Even the control of life is handed over

---

[2] The local hospital had a unit specifically set aside for psychiatric care and substance misuse which was known colloquially as "the psychy hut".

They can lock you up
tell you you're wrong thinking
pump you with drugs that take out your soul,
even do ECT[3] without your permission...
    fortunately for me at least that option was not taken up!
You can swear at them
scream "fuck you",
cry,
not speak.
It makes no difference
They are the doctors.
The professionals
You know nothing
They have the power and know best,
but what do they really know?
No-one really listened past the suicide crap
said "what do you know that will help?"
Sue: Which way do you want to go with this conversation?
I wonder..
We could talk about how you managed to escape that control, or what
difference you think that kind of question makes...?

Alex: I think in some ways they are both about the same thing.
I think what I discovered was a different kind of power,
not so much about them and us,
and the clash (hits knuckles together).
It was more of a side-stepping.
Of linking with others,
looking at different choices.
Looking at what I knew and ways I could know

---

[3] Electroconvulsive Therapy (ECT) is a psychiatric treatment sometimes given for
the treatment of severe depression, especially when other treatments have failed.
Its use is declining, but remains controversial. For more information see
www.mind.org.uk.

while they were trying to force me into a round hole and not
asking why I didn't fit
I just battered at them with the only way I know to get control,
trying to die.
To say to them
"I can do it and I will!"
You were very good at side-stepping and opening up different
doors which I could look through and choose
shall I go there?

Sue: (laughter) I'm wondering about this side-stepping
was that me avoiding a power struggle do you think?

Alex: I think I tried to engage you in the power struggle....
When I looked at the poems
I guess..
I know I was

abusive...

Sue: I could have walked away though – perhaps that was my power?

Alex: Yes you had your own power
but I realised that I didn't have to battle with you.
You were giving me freedom
I could look at things without wanting control.
What has always been important but sometimes impossible
is freedom.

Freedom to move,
and that's powerful too,
but also terrifying.
Perhaps what I wanted then,
and perhaps what I want now,
are services like mental health to be led by what people need

rather than what is thought "right".

I want those who assume "helping" roles
to listen to those who are hurting.

Sue: I've just been reading something written by a chap called Foucault he
says the same kind of thing.
Power should ascend rather than descend
It then means the institutions are controlled by those using them rather
than the other way round[4].... sorry....

Alex: I think there's something also about power and fear.
If the power and control between us is more equal there is less
fear.

If the power and control are one-sided then the other person
feels a high level of fear.

Because narrative approaches to both counselling and research come
from a perspective of seeing the person as the expert in their world and de-
centre[5] the counsellor (or researcher) seeing them as influential, but not
central to the process the traditional power structures and the subsequent
dilemmas are avoided as Alex so aptly put it we can sidestep onto a
different course.

If we see identity as constructed through relationship and the stories
we tell of our lives, then our identities can be re-authored (White 2007),
we can change the stories we live by and feel empowered by the process.

Lastly within this chapter I want to explore how looking at the
particularities of lived experience and seeing this as "knowledge" can
change the balance of power between the researcher and researched.

---

[4] White and Epston discuss Foucault's concept of power-the section I was referring
to can be found (White and Epston 1990:23-24)
[5] For more information about the de-centred position of the therapist within
narrative therapy approaches see White (2007)

Using narrative practices to side-step traditional structures of power and to explore the particularities of lived experiences

Power, knowledge and control Alex felt had everything to do with what happened to him both as a child and also within the mental health systems where he was treated. Side-stepping, looking at alternative stories of his life enabled him to relate to power and control in a different way and respected a different kind of knowledge.

Sidestepping within research settings can perhaps mean stepping from a culture of searching for "truth" and formulating theory and an overview of a particular issue or issues to one where the co-researchers zoom in on the particular in order to examine not just the issues and the stories and transform the mundane into the exotic (White 2004), but also illuminate the gaps and cracks between the stories to give new vistas of imagination, and new possibilities for redefining lives in ways that were not thought possible. Speedy states,

> "it is within the gaps and cracks that exist between these different stories that the liminal or threshold spaces in conversations, the points of entry to 'other' sites and identity performances begin to appear" (Speedy 2007:32)

Entering the field of research felt daunting, I could see the value to Alex and myself for undertaking this kind of research. It would I hoped enable me to audit my therapeutic practice, and Alex felt that for him it would be therapeutic. Sometimes however I questioned myself as to whether this type of research would be valuable to anyone else. If we were only looking with a magnifier at our own lives and ways of relating how could this be of any interest to anyone apart from ourselves? Surely research should be about generating knowledge?

There is something amazing about the power of personal stories however. Stories seem to breed stories (Bird 2000). I started to tell the stories of my work with Alex to audiences, and discovered that people would then approach me afterwards telling me of how what I had said resonated with their own life or work experiences. They would then tell me their own story. I received emails from counsellors telling me the stories of their experiences of working with suicidal clients, people would write telling me of their own feelings of despair and suicide and how they had escaped them. Linking our lives over common themes had given permission to talk about issues that were difficult to talk about in other settings, and also had somehow changed the way they thought and felt about their work and life.

Perhaps this kind of research is not about the researcher generating theory about a specific topic based on expert knowledge, but is more about enriching and thickening what is talked about and seen as relevant by the people who are at the centre of the research process, and increases the amount of local knowledge. This local knowledge can perhaps stand alongside more traditional knowledge and give more breadth and depth to our understanding of specific issues, particularly in the case of marginalised groups such as those using suicidal thoughts and feelings to cope with extreme emotional pain.

When we speak in terms of "providing services for" or "treating" particular groups of people, perhaps we need to think about what concerns the people we are servicing and how they view their needs. This means finding a way to give people a voice, and then listening to that voice. If we could do this successfully then surely this would then avoid both the traditional authoritarian styles of power and also the sometimes crippling normalization of social pressure of modern power as discussed earlier in this chapter.

Minorities can bring about changes in social and government policies if they link lives and create a collective voice. It was, after all, only a century ago that women got the right to vote, and this came about because of the growing pressure which could not be ignored, and the same is true for many groups who have in the past been marginalised by race, ability, religion or sexuality.

I have been thinking about community, and what this over-used word really means. Perhaps if we take it to mean "lives linked round common themes" (Myerhoff 1986) then the building of community can inform those who seek to provide services for others.

Traditionally research activities within counselling research assume that as Speedy points out "it is the counsellors not the clients who are researching therapeutic practice" (Speedy 2007:51), but what happens if we for a moment consider that some clients may wish to undertake research of their experience of counselling. This leads to a view of research from a very different perspective. How comfortable would we be

I wonder, if our clients routinely asked us to be participants in their research studies?

CHAPTER FOUR

NARRATIVELY SPEAKING

Introduction

Part one of this book has attempted to give the reader a backdrop against which my counselling and research conversations with Alex took place. It has looked at counselling and research ethics, how power, control, and knowledge have influenced our work and introduced Alex.

This chapter gives a specific introduction to the narrative that features in part two of the book. It starts with my first conversations with Alex about the possible research, then moves to exploring how the data collected by us (in the form of audio recordings of counselling sessions, written journals and notes from counselling and supervision sessions) have been transformed into the narrative text and explores how the act of writing the narratives constituted a new reality for both Alex and myself.

The beginnings of a research project

As discussed previously, if identity is seen as constructed through relationship, and the stories we tell of our lives, then the stories we tell during the therapeutic encounter will change how we view the world. When these are "written" as part of a research process, the meanings will again change and a new narrative emerges. In this instance this second narrative begins with our email conversations.

Neither this email narrative, or indeed the narrative of our counselling encounters, contains the "truth" about counselling suicidal clients or research, but will hopefully offer "useful ideas about how power, knowledge and 'truth' are negotiated" (Freedman and Combs 1996:22).

Email conversations with Alex
December 2004-January 2005

From: alex4research
Sent: 21 Dec 2004 09:04

Hi lol,
Have been giving some thought to this research. Yes. I hope that we can do
it. Last time it was good to spend time thinking, and I was amazed what we
came up with[1]. Yes I know you wrote it, but it sort of gave me a voice. I
don't think looking at the conversations will take me back anywhere that
will hurt me. Dying was my way of coping. You know getting control back
at that time. Now I've moved on and got better ways of coping- those
stories were me then, they are not me now. I'd like to know what went on.
Still not sure how talking through all that crap helped. I think that whether
you write it or not it is something that I am interested in doing. I've got a
desire for life now, and a woman (the best) and am now listening to others
wading through the shit[2]. Somehow sharing my stories about the shit mean
that others can know, "you can escape these stories". It may help people
listen more rather than say "yeurr *** this is too scary to work with".
Sometimes I think that I wasted all those years thinking about dying. If I
don't talk about them they will be just that pointless.If you need me to sign
something then it'll have to go in post.
Catch you later Alex
P.s. I'm happy to still be Alex. Those stories belong to Alex the real me is
more than they ever were.

From: dalesunnyplace
Sent: 05 Jan 2005 10.47

Hi Alex,
Thank you for the email-yes I hope that we can do it to. Have you any
ideas as to where we might start? Two years worth of conversations (69
sessions) is quite a lot of talking!
Sue

---

[1] One of the modules of the MSc course required that I write a case study relating
to one of my counselling clients. Instead of writing a traditional anonymous case
study from the perspective of the counsellor I asked Alex if he would be interested
in writing with me about his experience of counselling. The 5,000 word paper was
submitted as course work but not published.
[2] Alex was working at the time as a volunteer for a local drug and alcohol project
and was undertaking counselling training.

From: alex4research
Sent: 06 Jan 2005 09:28

Hi lol,
I have been looking through my journal from back then. I've sent you some stuff snail mail about when I was a child. You'll probably have to re-write it to make some kind of sense. Let me know.
Alex

From: dalesunnyplace
Sent: 08 January 2005 08:45

Hi Alex,
I am currently writing an essay proposing which research method would be helpful to use for the dissertation[3], how would you feel about me including your email (21 December) I attach draft copy of the essay-let me know whether it is ok to use this and the excerpt from transcript or whether you wish to change them or not use them.
All best wishes, Sue

From: alex4research
Sent: 09 Jan 2005 15:17

Hi lol,
Yes absolutely fine. I'm happy for you to use the emails, plus other comments. You can tidy email up if you like, if not as they are will be fine.
Alex

Doing the research: turning conversation into text

Writing will always be part of any research process, in that it is through the written word that research is disseminated and shared with interested others. The words on the page will inform others of our research, participants, methodology, and data. As Hooks (1994) points out;

---

[3] Undertaking a research project and producing a dissertation was required for MSc Counselling course.

the finished writing is important in that, "whatever cannot be written clearly cannot be used to educate" (hooks cited by Janesick 1999:505).

How we write, will be influenced by the audience to whom we are aiming to speak, and whether we see writing as merely recording the "truth" about the phenomenon that we are studying, or whether we consider the writing itself to be more than a recording tool, but creating a new different reality out of the words inscribed on the page. Richardson comments,

> "Language is not simply 'transparent', reflecting a social reality out there. Rather, language is a *constitutive* force, creating a particular view of language". (Richardson 1990:12).

If we see the writing as changing of reality, then the research process can be located within, and through the process of creation of the text, as well as, and not just, in our conversations with our participants. Even if we would prefer to think of the "writing up" of our research projects as merely reporting that which we have discovered, how we write, the particular phrases which words of our participants we choose to use will all "create a particular view of reality" (Richardson 1992:9) and will not fully represent all of the interactions between us and our participants, and will be a different reality from our original conversations with our participants.

As we write about the experience of our research we can learn about ourselves as well as our research topic (Richardson and Adams St. Pierre 2000:959). The process of writing can move us from one place of understanding to another. Hooks when speaking of her writing says:

> "Writing is my passion. It is a way to experience the ecstatic. The root of understanding of the word *ecstasy*-'to stand outside'-comes to me in those moments when I am immersed so deeply in the act of thinking and writing that everything else, even flesh, falls away" (Hooks 1999:35).

Who we are and what we are interested in will inevitably influence how we write. As Richardson points out,

> "the research self is not separable from the lived self. Who we are and what we can be, what we can study, and how we can write about what we study are all tied to how a knowledge system disciplines its members and claims authority over knowledge" (Richardson 2003:197).

If we agree that writing does create different realities from those of our interactions and conversations with our participants, the ethical dilemma becomes how then can we represent the words of others spoken to us in the context of research in ways that represent the reality the participant wants to convey? It is not enough to merely present their words spoken out of context.

Josselson comments that: "Language can never contain a whole person, so every act of writing a person's life is inevitably a violation" (Josselson 1996:62), and I am mindful of this as I transcribe our (Alex and my) words on to the page. "The ability to provide multiple opportunities for 'voice' in privileged settings, without further marginalizing a group or individual" (Chapman 2005:27) is one of the challenges to those writing about other people who consider themselves to be on the margins of society (where Alex and I believe having conversations about suicide has placed us). As our experience is inscribed within the academic it seems we move from the margins to the centre and find a voice.

I had, as stated earlier, data from several different sources including recordings kept by Alex of our counselling sessions. My first task was to transcribe these and find a way of representing the conversations and stories told on paper. I then turned to the journals Alex kept at the time of our counselling sessions (which were mainly in poetic narrative) and my journal, and notes relating to counselling and supervision (which were in prose) to see how I could make some kind of narrative that would make sense to a reader.

Cixous (1997) comments that "what sets me writing is that lava, the flesh, that blood, those tears: they are in all of us" (Cixous and Calle Gruber 1997:11). She is describing writing as a process of inquiry, and that it is "in the writingness [ecruance] itself, in the material, in the course of the writing, I am already in the process of shaking all this up" (Cixious and Calle:11). The transcribing of text is often seen as tedious and to be avoided, and not really "writing" at all, but there is something important for me in the laborious listening, typing and re-listening. It gives me deeper re-call and memory of the original conversation and it is the setting down of the words onto paper that is the beginning of the process of writing, the beginning of the "process of shaking all this up" (Cixious and Calle:11).

As stated previously, text in whatever form, no matter how accurately transcribed, cannot fully represent the conversation which it articulates. The dynamics of the moment held between the individuals involved is far too complex to capture in words. These words however are starting points, a map of the terrain.

To give the reader some idea of the process what follows next is a small excerpt of the transcript of one of the audio recordings of our conversations:

Excerpt transcript 3
Sue: When you talk about that…I mean..It em… sounds like ….

Alex: I meant to go that night…I wasn't just being dramatic or anything like that. I was calm, and I wrote letters. Em.. you know. I even made a will……Just couldn't stand the pain anymore…….

Sue: you couldn't stand it any more…..

Alex: No… (laughter) I listened to Led Zep on the car recorder and had taken about half the booze and this …paracetemols when I got it in my head to phone her.

Sue: You phoned her…. so you changed your mind?

Alex: Yes I phoned her, can't remember quite….Such a stupid git. Why phone her..stupid thing…I drifted in and out can't really remember much. You know. In and out of ….Peaceful – for a time peaceful… I can't remember much more about that it all sort of blurs into a haze. When I came to I was vomiting over a vengeful nurse in the local hospital.

As I hold the map (transcript) and listen to the words again (and again) the next task is to start to draw out the important words, the ones stressed by the speaker, the gaps, the silences. I listen for the "talk that sings" (Bird 2004:4). The talk that evokes an emotive response, the stories that capture my imagination, this connects with my relationships with being a musician[4]. As Cixous says:

> "There is a sort of extraordinary, sublime universality of music. A part of my work has its source in the same material. The sonorous material. To write is to note down the music of the world, the music of the body, the music of time" (Cixous and Calle-Gruber 1997:46).

As I start the transcription process, I am aware that I have started to make "choices based on the theories (I) hold" (Etherington 2000:292). I will make the decisions on which sections to use, and will suggest how to represent the transcription within text. Listening again to the transcript I highlight and emphasise the words that seem to "sing":

Excerpt transcript 3

Sue: When you talk about that…I mean..It em… sounds like ….

Alex: I meant to go that night…I wasn't just being dramatic or anything like that. I was calm, and I wrote letters. Em.. you know. I even made a will……Just couldn't stand the pain anymore…….

Sue: you couldn't stand it any more?

Alex: No… (laughter) I listened to Led Zep on the car recorder and had taken about half the booze and this …paracetemols when I got it in my head to phone her.

Sue: You phoned her…. so you changed your mind?

Alex: Yes I phoned her, can't remember quite….Such a stupid git. Why phone her..stupid thing…I drifted in and out …can't really remember much. You know. In and out of ….Peaceful – for a time peaceful… I can't remember much more about that it all sort of blurs into a haze. When I came to I was vomiting over a vengeful nurse.

---

[4] Prior to working as a counsellor I had worked in schools as a peripatetic flute teacher.

I am aware that the transcription (both the audio recording and the text) is not the same as the conversation in itself, it is not merely a re-telling of something that has already happened (Lapadat and Lindsay 1999 cited by Etherington 2000). Since having my original conversation with Alex the world for both of us has changed, and if we spoke again now we would not utter the same words. Just as when this book is published it too will be only a partial historical reflection of our story at this time, not an accurate representation of how it is for us at the time you read it.

Listening to the transcript again I take out the highlighted words and place them on a new page and change the font: to the one Alex says he prefers.

A poem emerges. "What is most true is poetic. What is most true is naked life. I can only attain this mode of seeing with the aid of poetic writing" (Cixous and Calle-Gruber 1997:4).

I meant to go that night
I wasn't just being dramatic
I was calm
I wrote letters, made a will.
Just couldn't stand the pain anymore.
I listened to Led Zep on the car recorder and had taken
about half the booze and paracetemols
when I got it in my head to phone her.

Stupid git
I drifted in and out
Peaceful – for a time peaceful
When I came to I was vomiting over a vengeful nurse

If poetry is defined by rhythm, structure, resonance, and is evocative and as Bachelard (1964) points out exists in sound within its resonance and reverberation (Bachelard cited in Behan 2003), conversation also has these qualities. We do not speak as we would write, and do not use the formal grammatical prose of which written documents (this book included) are composed, but our words as we speak them are also defined by rhythm, structure and resonance especially it seems when we are speaking of things which are important to us. As Tedlock (1983) writes,

"If anthropologists, folklorists, linguists, and oral
historians
are interested in the full meaning
of the spoken word
then they must stop treating oral narratives
as if they were reading prose
when in fact they are listening to dramatic poetry" (Tedlock 1983:123)

Social Science researchers such as Richardson (1990; 2000), Behan (1999; 2003), Etherington (2000), Hill (2005), Speedy (2007) have used poetic stanzas to create evocative accounts of social behaviour. Behan describes this poetic form as "rescued speech poems" commenting that when we talk this is not in the prose common to text, but within the emotive language of the poet (Behan 2003). Hill states:

"Poetry can make situations more vivid to the reader. It provides us with a window into the feelings of characters, and it encapsulates the essence of events that many of us have lived at one time or another" (Hill 2005:95).

Speedy speaks of how "poetry is perhaps less 'official', more intimate, more succinct and often presents a distillation of meanings that surprises and heartens people" (Speedy 2005:286). Placing Alex's words within a "poetic" document also seems in itself to be an "act of resistance" (Kristeva 1974 cited by Speedy 2005:286). This is perhaps resistance against the prejudices and marginalisation of people who are normally "patients" without a voice, and resistance against academic research that often appears to value the voice of the researcher over that of the researched.

Introduction to the narratives

Alex and I debated whether to present the text in two parallel columns alongside each other. His story on one side, mine on the other, but I felt that this did not give a clear indication of how the stories impacted on each other, and could be confusing and time consuming to read.

I wanted Alex's story to be the dominant theme throughout the narrative; it was after all an account of conversations placed within a context of a counselling relationship that had placed his story firmly in the centre of the process. I decided therefore with Alex's agreement to use text boxes to confine my own story and place these within the text of Alex's narrative. I consider this reflected my counselling role where I strived to create a genuine relationship where the process was transparent, and where my own feelings and thoughts were acknowledged and, where appropriate, shared with the client in what Wosket (1999) describes as the "therapeutic use of self" (Wosket 1999:11). These were not however conversations about me, but about Alex. At times my own story does impact on Alex's as can be seen in how the text box displaces the stanzas which represent his story. At times my story helps move Alex's story into a richer fuller description. At other times it is shown as disruptive, breaking up Alex's text. Speedy has given thought to presentation of multi-layered narratives within research papers, and comments of her own presentation of narrative accounts "the stories have been positioned together across the landscape in order to speak visually of some of the kaleidoscopic possibilities that exist alongside each other in conversation" (Speedy 2005:70). It is my hope that the following narratives will not only speak to the reader in the words of the text, but also visually as they interweave.

As the research process unfolded another narrative came into being, told out through email conversation. This has also been included and is our "research story". I concluded that these email conversations enriched the original stories giving fresh insight and encouraged dialogue with, and "fuller descriptions of the original stories" (White 2003:3).

Finally I wanted to finish this section by considering some of the objectives that Alex and I had both in undertaking the research and also for turning what was an academic dissertation into a book.

When Alex and I contemplated undertaking the research project we shared, both joint, and individual objectives. Firstly we were both interested in creating a narrative which was experiential, something to which the reader could respond. Indeed we wished to create resonances within wider communities which would create thicker, richer descriptions of a subject matter that is seen by many as "taboo", and give voice to marginalised individuals who use suicidal thoughts and behaviours to cope with extreme psychological pain. This has also been very important when considering a publication that would be available for larger audiences.

One of Alex's main aims was to give a voice to what he considered "the unspeakable conversations" and to give hope to those others "wading through the shit" that "you can escape these stories[5] and this is was an important factor in him supporting publication.

From a personal perspective when I first approached Alex about research possibilities it was in order to audit my therapeutic practice to see what as a counsellor I was doing well, and discover what was missing. I had over the years worked alongside many individuals who felt that suicide was the only solution, and I wanted to understand firstly what was helpful and unhelpful in my practice. I also wanted to give voice to the ethical and emotional dilemmas counsellors may encounter when working with these kinds of conversations, and to see if any of my personal stories of suicide had any connection with the way I worked. The project did indeed highlight many aspects of my therapeutic practice, both helpful and unhelpful, and as a result my counselling practice has changed[6]. It has also informed my practices as a supervisor and trainer, publication of these stories to wider audiences will hopefully engage other counsellors in conversation about these issues.

Our reasons for undertaking the research project at that particular time (2004) were different[7]. For me it was part of my coursework for an MSc award. For Alex it was to gain personal insight. As discussed in chapter one, I have strived to ensure the research was collaborative, and my motives and methods were transparent, but I do recognise that the MSc criteria did influence my editorial decisions, and I did choose, albeit in consultation with Alex, which parts of the stories to include or exclude. There was also the matter of which ex-client I chose to undertake this project with, as Etherington points out, "our role provides us with the power to choose whose voices will be heard" (Etherington 2000:263). After all I have worked with many clients who have had suicidal thoughts, and they may also have wanted to have the opportunity to develop their own voice. It has felt a powerful position one that I am not always comfortable with. I can only hope that my decisions to include or exclude have not had a detrimental affect on those whom I have had conversations with in the past. I feel deeply indebted to everyone who has shared stories of their lives with me and consider that all the stories have left an imprint within me and changed who I am and how I relate to people, and indeed what I have written within this book.

---

[5] see email 21st December shown earlier in this chapter
[6] You will find a fuller description of these changes in chapters nine and ten.
[7] See Alex's email on page 84

PART 2:

ENGAGING WITH SUICIDE: THE NARRATIVES

CHAPTER FIVE

DAWN

Journal 7th January 2000
I sit here at the beginning of a millennium year thinking about that
night (now over ten years ago) and my feelings as I sat in the dark,
wanting just for it to swallow me up. I was so tired of struggling, of
crying, of fighting. I loved my children so much, yet felt alienated from
being with them by self-blame and hate. I watched as the sky became
lighter, the sun rising from behind the opposite hill, and it was one of
those moments which stand still in the memory. A moment of numinous
otherness. It was as if someone or something was holding out a light to
me and saying, "however dark the night is, dawn will always come".
There was a certainty a sense of wonder, and wisdom. I could face
whatever there was in the future. I chose to walk forward in faith.

In retrospect this was a turning point in my life. It enabled me to move
forward in life, to face whatever had to be faced, to look into the dark
of night knowing that dawn would always come. Dawn continues to be
a metaphor which has shaped both my personal response to despair,
and also my work with those despairing of life itself. I keep a
photograph of "dawn over Bron-yr-Aur" in my study. A reminder to
keep hope and faith.

Introduction

Using suicidal thoughts and behaviours as a way of coping with
extreme psychological (or even physical) pain is as discussed previously,
not that uncommon. Many of us at some time in our life will have some
thought (even if fleeting and not acted on) about whether life is really
worth living, usually at times when few choices seem to exist, or when
everything seems out of our control and we feel trapped. Even small
children feel that sometimes "life" is all they have control over. As

Speedy's research participants "the unassuming geeks" (who are a group connected by suicide) write:

"Thinking of others for a moment,
as a very small boy,
he could keep himself alive and
hopeful by thinking
that he still had the power of breath.
How did he know so much?

Thinking of others for a moment.
He and no one else
had control of his breathing.
It was his body, his diaphragm,
and he could make it breathe, or not." (Speedy 2005:130)

Alex had used suicidal thoughts and behaviours, since childhood, as a way of coping with extreme psychological pain but he now wanted to find different ways of coping and to find better ways of describing his life.

Together we co-researched the "thoughts" beginnings, their history, and how they had kept him feeling "in control" and "safe" at times when the only thing he did have control of was life itself. It is these beginnings that make up this first chapter.

The emphasis within all of my therapeutic work is that the client is the "expert" in their world, and my task is to stand alongside as a co-researcher and see the person as separate from the problem. In theory this sounds fairly routine practice for a narrative counsellor, and appears a respectful and empowering way of working. When faced with a client who is suicidal however this stance is not nearly so straightforward. I wanted to stay with Alex and how these "thoughts" had affected his life but, as discussed previously, there were also questions of professional responsibilities, organisational responsibilities, and the knowledge that these problem "thoughts" could end his life.

Within the narrative I have tried to show visually how my own anxieties about the work impeded on Alex's story. Sometimes you will see that my interjections (shown in text boxes) facilitate his story, other times they squeeze his story into small spaces, and at some times they take over completely.

Alex: February-April 2000

I imagine a place where I can just be.
Without this agony – this hell.

Peace

No more tearing wrenching grinding.
A place of non-being where the out of control-ness
of being on a grain of sand on a rollercoaster

STOPS

I decide.

> Session notes 11th February 2000
> *I struggle not to go into rescue mode.*
> *Feel surrounded by his despair.*
> *There is no escape.*

I fantasize about what
this place will look like
How it will be.

Will it be anything or nothing?
Nothing seems preferable.

How I might get there?
The planning is meticulous.
It gives me something concrete to do, to think about,
I am in control of this.
No-one can take away
what goes on in my head.

If I start to get stressed with one plan,
There is always another to take its place.

Then sometimes

I get scared.
The thoughts take over

have a life
of their own.

Session notes 18th February 2000
"A" reported taking an overdose of prescription drugs during the week, he just wanted to die. But he had "woken up again". We talked about his feelings of hate, which terrify him. "It feels as if they will consume me" he says. Urged him to have a check up with his GP.

Then they are in
control

NOT ME.

HELP!

Need to talk-it is
too crap to think
about.
There must be
another way?

The main theme seems to be "despair", he talks also of his acute feelings of fear and loneliness, my own feelings mirror his. I too am close to being consumed by the chaos.

I am really concerned for this person – what can I do?

The guardians of
my health say:

"NO
you mustn't even
think like that-what sort of man are you anyway?

Session notes 25th February 2000
"Life is just too hard" "A" says. He asks me to look after prescription drugs as he is frightened to have them in the house in case he takes them all. He "craves oblivion". He can't articulate more than single words, and his whole body shakes.

WHAT
WOULD
YOUR MUM
SAY?"

*We agree that drugs will be handed over for safe keeping to pharmacy. The risk of suicide is **high**, client agrees I may speak to his GP. I feel very angry. GP not very interested "ok. I'll note it down. He's always making suicide attempts, the mental health team can't do any more" he says. Where does that leave me?*

Guilt upon
guilt

burden
so heavy.

My tears, of self-loathing
make it easier to act on,
but then again

I'm out of control.
Go on end it the voice in my head sneers.

Session notes 3rd March 2000
"A" talks again of the pointlessness of his life. I feel desperately
sad. It would be such a waste if he committed suicide. He has
fought against so much for so long. Am I getting too close?

At the end of the session I offer an extra appointment "I will be
there" he says. I feel relieved by these words and humbled that so
little could matter so much to him.

They drag me back, lock me away,

I scream inside

No-one hears

The drugs stop the words in my throat.
Keep quiet the thoughts say. Keep quiet, bide time plan.
THE JUDAS TREE WAITS
they can't take that away.

Supervision notes 14th March 2000
Main Areas of Learning from the supervision on this client

What I have learnt about my client:
1)   Client may deliberately, or accidentally commit suicide
2)   He is searching for meaning to life which could include
      "spiritual dimension".
3)   At times he struggles desperately for life and a way through at
      other times he wants to give up.
4)   I need to inform GP if I am concerned for his safety.

What I have learnt about myself:
1) *How vulnerable I feel working with and staying with his deep despair and desire for death as a solution.*
2) *How much my counselling was affected by my own stress (moving house). Although on the surface I coped as usual there was somehow less of me available for the other.*
3) *That it is ok to stay with the chaos despite wanting at times to avoid the clients despair.*
4) *Sometimes I like this client, at other times I dislike him, but I can live (& work) with this ambivalence and still be "for" him. How I will think/work with this client now:*

I will ensure that very firm boundaries are adhered to. I will continue to stay with him in the chaos, but when appropriate challenge and keep my own perspective on reality. I will encourage him towards appropriate self-help groups. Counselling should encourage him back into community rather than replace all other social contact. Where possible I will glean information about his early life and development as this may be the key to understanding what is going on behind the presenting problems.

I suppose it started when I was about 6 or 7

it was this place I could go to in my head

Session notes 17th March 2000
So relieved when he walks through the door.

that no-one knew about.

No-one could touch me there.
My secret.

At school I peed myself
I remember being stood on

a chair.

Humiliation.

Everyone's eyes on me,
hating everyone looking.
This one lad screwed up his nose

STINK!
He called me stink

always for
years.

Session notes 31st March 2000

> *Session notes 31ˢᵗ March 2000*
> *Return to sessions after my house move. I feel he is making small talk to avoid talking about painful issues. Perhaps I should have reflected this back using "immediacy" but my gut reaction was to go with the flow. In retrospect I believe that I was actually trying to avoid his chaos because:*
>
> 1) *Coping with his, as well as my own turmoil (re moving) seemed too much.*
> 2) *Taking time off feels too risk-I am afraid for his safety.*
>
> *Am I taking too much responsibility for his life? I will take this to supervision.*

STINK THIS
STINK
THAT

I remember
not being able
to bear
being there.

Wanting just
to disappear.

In the moment all those
eyes on me.

Being uncomfortable
sore between the legs.
My trousers stiff like card
and then somehow wishing I wasn't..

WISHING

wishing, I wasn't there.

Wondering

if I stopped breathing perhaps I'd die.
It kept me from being up there on the chair.
I must have stood there for about 20 minutes,
I suppose it could have been a year.
I lay in bed that night
practicing holding my breath,
got so angry that I just couldn't stop,
just couldn't stop breathing.

Journal 31ˢᵗ March 2000
Listening to this story from "A". I rage at God.
How could a loving God allow this to happen?

What had this child ever done to deserve such
treatment?

I cried

why couldn't I
stop breathing.
Why?

Later I thought up all manner of plans,

I snuck away all mums carvers and
sharpened them.
God – she looked everywhere for them!
I looked at it every night
I felt it
you know..
so powerful.

Even the spitting and the other stuff
didn't touch me,
I went to this..

God, I feel so ashamed telling you all this crap.
I need to talk though.

How can I keep telling?

So hard

do you hate me?
I can't bear to have you hearing this

Session notes 31st March 2000 *I'm aware of tears in my eyes but I keep* *looking, staying with him the best I can.*	**BUT DON'T LOOK** **AWAY THOUGH.** She hated me,

beat me for soiling my clothes.

WHY DID SHE DO THAT?
WHAT EVER DID I DO THAT WAS SO TERRIBLE?

I used to try to keep awake all night
so I didn't soil the sheets.
Sometimes I squeezed myself under the bed
It felt safe there.

I could go to this place in my head when I was there,
somewhere I was in control,
MY PLACE.

Session notes 12th April 2000
I felt so angry as "A" spoke. Why did
no-one notice what was going on? He
finds it hard to talk, says he feels
ashamed. I check with him what I can
do to make the telling more possible.
"Just be there, keep looking at me" he
says.

It was a place where I
decided whether I would
live or not,
I could end it anytime it
got too much.
MY PLACE.

It got better.
I stopped peeing myself

then ..

I went away to school.
At least before it was predictable,
at school you never knew
when someone would hit you,
or stick shit in your pocket,
or pin you down,
I became **vigilant.**
Hyper-vigilant.

Still am I suppose
always watching people,
getting them on my side,
I still had the place.
Yes.

No-one knew.
Knives were cool
so my knife was ok.
Occasionally I lost it
cut my leg
laughed and said..

God I can't say this..

NO-ONE NOTICED
Why did no-one notice?
Invisibility

I thought invisible
thoughts,
and no-one knew.

> *Supervision notes 14th April 2000*
> *We talked about how abuse, and suicide are "taboo" subjects, society doesn't want to hear about them. Talking about these experiences breaks the silence and enables new stories of life to emerge.*

Talking about this is so hard,

but liberating.
Somehow wish you'd been there then.

Why didn't
someone ask me then?
How has it taken so many fucking years to talk?

The secret place though was so important
It meant most of the time I could be normal

NORMAL

normal
whatever that is?

Session notes 16th April 2000
As "A" spoke he became very angry. I encouraged him to stay with the feelings. So often he has been told his feelings are inappropriate. This felt to me like a very appropriate feeling.

I couldn't have survived
without that place
It was the only thing that
kept me from ceasing to
exist.

You know you are alive when you bleed
and if you can't just
stop breathing
you have to do something to die.
That means that you're alive.
Telling just rambling like this does the same.

Email received 18 April 2000
Hi Lol,
Today's session scary-surreal. I talked of when I was a kid. The humiliating degrading things, but it wasn't about these things really, it was about sharing a way I coped. I've always felt I fucked up as a kid. Hearing myself talk about it I felt, sorry I

suppose, for that kid. You didn't say a lot, but there were tears in your eyes I think. You cared about that kid. Me. That made it ok.

Regards Alex

I exist
I'm not invisible
which is scary,
but makes living possible, perhaps..

Oh shit this talking is so hard.
I want you to listen
But I'm..

AFRAID
If I'm not invisible..
I have to be
alive.
Not sure what this means.

I suppose it's a door that's always been there,
for so long anyway.
A familiar corridor and the speed to get there is:
flash
you're there.
I used always to get there without thinking.

NOW
I have time.
I have created the space.
If I go there it's a conscious decision, and that feels
POWERFUL.
I suppose like an alcoholic the booze is always there waiting,
beckoning,

It's seductive.
"COME IN YOU WILL BE HAPPY HERE"

Session notes 23rd April 2000
Feel really scared, cold all over.
As "A" spoke I felt a strong
desire to run. I am out of my
depth, entering a world I don't
understand I am not sure I can do

My hand rests on the door
latch
sensations fill me
like orgasmic,
a need to be fulfilled.
I hesitate at the door anticipation
of meeting a lover,
same kind of thoughts
"have I got the condoms?"
or in this case tablets, booze, knife – whatever.

Supervision notes 26th April 2000
We spent most of my supervision
session talking about my feelings
when I am with "A". "Do you want
to carry on working with him? If
you do, you need to go to that
'trapped' place and walk there with
him. Can you do that?" Asks Colin
[my counselling supervisor].

Just sitting staring at
the blade,

running my fingers over
it.
So hard to move my
concentration away.

I've learnt that putting
barriers in front of the door is

Journal 28th April 2000
It's strange "A" spoke about feeling "trapped". "Trapped" is also
how I feel sometimes when I'm with him. My emotions are mirroring
*his, except I can walk away, and **sometimes I want to**.*

USELESS
fucking useless.

In a moment like a madman I can tear them down.

Like the alcoholic who
tries to live never seeing alcohol.
Just one advert too much, he's there again.
Consumed by this madness,
this self-hate.
Loathing,
wanting to obliterate destroy.
Reject everything,
especially the trapped.

Like an orgy of anger.
It ends, as it always ends these days,
in A & E
being stitched without anaesthetic.
Throwing up in a bucket

Journal 30th April 2000
I was nervous today as I approached the
Quiet Room. It took all my will-power to
open the door. I was the first in the
building. What's that all about? I ask
myself. Possibly it's linked to "A's"
frequent comments about "hanging from
the beams". He brought a rope in last
week and although he seemed very
positive I couldn't take my thoughts
away from it. He said it was for tying up
some garden rubbish, but it seemed to
burn an image on my brain which I can't
get rid of.

HATING
TRAPPED.

Not sure I should have
said so much.

Feel down today.

When I think about it
that kid was ok,
I just wish I could
believe it.

Sue says she wasn't upset with me for thinking like I did.
So many folks have said

I've got wrong thinking.
So it's kind of hard to believe her.

I always feel kind of shit scared as I walk up the stairs towards
that room[1].

It means so much
that room.
I picture it in my mind
the beams,
the stones and shells.
But walking towards it I get the stomach churning
sweaty hands
want to run.

Surely as a man I shouldn't be saying
this crap?
I'm not sure why it is ok to talk here,
the beams are so old, strong.
It would be a good place to die here
Sue would find me.
I worry sometimes about not being found.
Just rotting away
somewhere.
Sometimes I want to keep talking and talking to get it all out;
I can't believe being heard.
Sometimes I'm so scared because I need Sue so much.
She could and will walk away anytime,
I mean nothing to her, it's just her work.

I hate her for that.
She and her bloke probably have a good laugh when she gets
home
Yet when she's here she doesn't laugh..

---

[1] The Quiet Room was the counselling room used by myself and a colleague. It
was in the attic of an old building attached to a city centre church. It had a number
of exposed cross beams which stretched across the room holding the walls apart.

> *Session notes 30th April 2000*
> *"A" seemed to be avoiding talking;*
> *he spent much of the time speaking*
> *about the problems with his car. It*
> *felt as if he was avoiding painful*
> *issues.*

I shouldn't need
anyone.

Wonder sometimes why
she does it?
Perhaps she's a "sicko"
who gets off on
listening to men
cracking up.
I ran up the stairs today.
Couldn't wait to be sitting there talking,
being with someone who cared
And when I got there, I couldn't say anything.

Why am I such a stupid git?

I DON'T DESERVE TO LIVE

Email Conversations about Research
January – March 2005

From: alex4research
Sent: 30 Jan 2005 15:32

Hi lol,
Have just sent you some more journal stuff thru snail mail. It's strange, at
the time some of the stuff we talked about was just so difficult to say. I
suppose it's because I had never talked about it before, or because when I
had, people reacted taking away my rights and saying I shouldn't think like
that. Now when I look at it is just part of my past. I was looking through
some of the stuff about me as a boy and I was kind of proud. How amazing
for such a small kid to find such a brilliant way of escaping the crap and
humiliation of what was going on. Now instead of feeling ashamed (which
I did when we talked about it) and that it was my fault, and that I was dirty,
not worthy of anyone I feel angry. Good anger. Angry not so much with
the other kids but angry with the teachers. Why did they do it? They were
deliberately sadistic. I was talking about it to (name deleted) the other
night, and she is (or was) a teacher for many years, and she says it

wouldn't happen now, and if it did there would be people to talk to about it. I'm not sure that I believe her, I think on the whole that there will always be sadistic buggers around in any profession. I am glad though that less kids will have to put up with such treatment.

I am talking about this stuff to (name of therapist) he says that it is really good that I've moved so far. Thank you for taking my tales so seriously both then and now.
Alex

From: dalesunnyplace
Sent: 01 Feb 2005 09:11

Hi Alex,
Thank you for the email. It sounds as if how you remember those memories has changed a lot. Are you sure that you still want to go on with this? I don't want you to feel obligated to go back anywhere that is difficult.
All best wishes, Sue.

From: alex4research
Sent: 04 Feb 2005 23:24

Hi lol,
Thanks for the draft proposal and email.

First I feel like saying "for Gods sake get a grip". I am undertaking this project for my reasons not yours. I want to find out more about our conversations. They changed life for me I think exploring them through research will be therapeutic. You do not have to take responsibility for me I am happy to take responsibility for my own actions. Already I am changing- thinking about it and that's really good. I have plenty of support. Don't worry, use the emails if you need to. The examiner wants to make sure you are not harming me. **No you are not.** I know what I am signing up for, and want to do it.
Take care of yourself. Alex

From: dalesunnyplace
Sent: 04 Feb 2005 19:15

Hi Alex,

Thank you, and I'm sorry. I think I'm getting the wobbles and that's not about you or your commitment, but my stuff about not being a "good researcher" or a "good counsellor". Also perhaps about suicide being such a taboo subject, and us putting our conversations out there for all to see. I think you should say, "for God's sake get a grip" and I think I am (or trying to).

Thanks again. I know you are capable of taking responsibility.
All best wishes Sue

From: alex4research
Sent: 04 February 2005 19:27

Hi lol,
Thanks for the email. Suicide is a difficult one. I think that what I'm interested in is exploring my stuff, it's like I can work through it again and tell my story and that feels great. I care about your research, but it's not my priority. I know as well that my identity will not be known, I can tell people if I want to but you have put your name on this thing, and it is you who will be judged, so perhaps the "wobbles" are ok.

Anyway I've dug out some more stuff and sent it to you snail-mail.
Speak to you soon Alex

From: dalesunnyplace
Sent: 06 Feb 2005 08:35

Hi Alex,
I'm interested in finding out more about what your priorities are and how you would envisage your story looking like in this research. Sue

---

From: alex4research
Sent: 07 Feb 2005 10:47

Hi lol,
Just switched on the computer to your messages.

I think the priority for me is having my story told, and seeing it in writing in a way that is ok for me. I don't think it's anymore than that.

Talking about it to you and others has been really life changing. Now I want to somehow see it down on paper. I'm interested in your side of it, but that for me isn't the priority. I'm interested in what it is about our conversations that made it good, but again this is not the priority.

I guess what I'd like is for you to write it down for me and for me to add or take out bits not relevant, or that would identify me or others. Would that give you enough for you to do the rest of what you want?
Alex

From: dalesunnyplace
Sent: 21 February 2005 09:32

Hi Alex, hope all is well with you.

I have attached an initial draft of your early memories about suicidal thoughts.

I have used your journal, plus my counselling notes. I have not changed the wording into narrative form, because I thought that it would be more effective to use your own words. If you don't like it presented in this way we can think again. If there are any bits you would rather not use, or if you want to re-draft it then do. This is your story! You need to think about whether other people you mention will be affected by what is written, or whether this will make it hard for you to remain anonymous.
All best wishes Sue

From: alex4research
Sent: 22 Feb 2005 23:21
Hi lol,
For once words escape me.

Seeing it wrote there. It's like a poem yet not. It's strange although I know the story so well. Been through it a million times seeing it there on the page makes it feel real. You know, it really happened to that kid. He was me. I can almost reach out and touch him. Why was no-one there for him. Why was he treated like shit? I suppose I'll never get the answers to that one. You said to me once that he was brilliant to have found a way of escaping and I suppose seeing it there on the page I can accept that.

If I had kids what would they be like I wonder? I wish there had been some other way though. Showed it to (name) she hugged me that was enough.

I think that perhaps I had better leave out the bit about me ma. I was very angry when I said it, but now I don't feel like that, and it sort of not my place to write about her when she can't respond. Is that ok?

Catch you later Alex

From: dalesunnyplace
Sent: 26 Feb 09:17

Hi Alex, thank you for the email.

It is strange, seeing the words on the paper was very powerful. You are right, he was an amazing kid. I don't know that there are any answers as to why he was treated in the way he was. Seeing the words on the paper I wanted to reach out and touch him. When we talked about it I remember feeling so sad that he was so alone, and angry with the adults, why didn't they notice what was going on?

Reading it now I am still sad and angry that a child had to endure so much, but I am amazed at how brilliantly he coped with unbearable pain.

I will make the amendments you suggest, and will send you the next instalment soon. Sue

---

From: alex4research
Sent: 07 March 2005 09:29

Hi lol,

Thanks. I suppose the difficult bit at the time of our conversations was the shame. I felt so damned ashamed of myself. I remember not being able to look at your face. I wanted to run out of the room. I know you would not judge me, but to have any person that close to know stuff about me made me shit scared. Now it's different I lift up my head. I can look you in the eyes now I spoke about it to (name), it was easy, doesn't take away all the pain but it doesn't have any hold over me now. Sometimes perhaps I'll write down the other crap about my childhood (not yet)but at least I know that the time will come when I can.

Is this going to be the first bit you use?

Regards Alex

From: dalesunnyplace
Sent: 08 March 2005 08:41

Yes, I think there will be some kind of introduction, and then this will make up the first section of the narrative. I thought that I would use it as is, with excerpts from my journals alongside. My initial thought is that I will split the narrative into four sections dawn, midday, dusk and night.

How does that sound? Sue

CHAPTER SIX

MIDDAY

Introduction

As the song says it is "only mad dogs and Englishmen that go out in the midday sun"[1] this, and indeed perhaps the title of the book (where angels fear to tread) allude to my ambivalent attitude towards writing about this subject matter. There is a part of me which is drawn to keep silent. There is fear in exposing both Alex, and my practice, to possible criticism. I am not only visible as "researcher" but "researched", and do not have the anonymity this role usually brings.

It is difficult to know the exact time that I became aware of suicide and what the word meant. Was it when I was seven and a distant cousin was discussed by the aunts over morning coffee in hushed tones in terms of "what a waste" and "how could he do something so awful", or when my father talked of the "bloody Jap's" who, "didn't value anyone's life let alone their own". Or was it in the moving Remembrance Day services with trumpets and solemnity when the young men who had, "given up their lives" for others were glorified.

I suppose the reality dawned when I was sixteen and my friend's father took an overdose of anti-depressants and died (whether by accident or suicide will never be known).

As a teenager he was just another old man (forty-two) who, when up and about was a vibrant part of family life, but spent much of his time "depressed" which to me (at that time) meant sitting quietly, not joining in conversations and spending many hours in bed. I accepted the strangeness of these mood swings, as teenagers do, with little thought. The reality of his death was shocking though. The family stunned, grieving, spoke of their attempts at reviving him. His children were alone with him the night

---

[1] This is the title of a well known song by Noel Coward (1931)

he died. The mixture of grief, anger, and disbelief rocked the foundations of the world in which I lived. I sat with them in their grief; as life closed in.

I remember in the long days between death and the funeral walking with the younger children to the local shops. The silence as we entered was overwhelming. No-one giving eye contact, no-one wanting to serve us. Suicide (or even the possibility of it) in this village, it seemed, was considered a "mortal sin". The angry words of his brother as apportioned blame. The empty words at the crematorium. The feeling of being tarnished with shame. The feeling of rejection, he rejected these beautiful wonderful people. My anger at this abandonment.

Years later, sitting on a cold Welsh hill staring into the blackness, I remember this man, and wonder about his level of his despair. I comprehend finally what depression is like and the desire to want to escape from the excruciating pain that is life.

Listening to Alex's historic accounts of suicidal thoughts and behaviours was one thing; I was affected by what I heard, as I am always when people talk to me of traumatic happenings in their past. At times vivid images haunted my thoughts and dreams.

Conducting a counselling relationship with someone who is constantly talking about wanting to die in the "here and now" however is very different. There are a myriad of feelings; sadness, anger, and most frequently fear; what will happen if this person does choose to die? What will I feel? What will other people say? Have I considered all the ethical implications? Should I have done more?

Being in a relationship with someone who is suicidal feels at times like madness, as does writing about it, but like either a "mad dog" or the English woman which I am, I am prepared to sit out exposed, in the heat of the midday sun, in the hope of adding to the small but growing research into the experiences and dynamics of conversations about suicide.

Email Conversations about Research
March 2005

From: dalesunnyplace
Sent: 12 March 2005 16:41
Hi Alex,
It was good to speak with you on the phone. I have amended the early memories as we talked about (see attached). There is still time to change things if you want to.

Thank you for the batch of journal entries, are you ready for me to start typing them up? If so, I propose to use the same kind of style as I did for the early memories. Would that feel ok?
All best wishes Sue

From: alex4research
Sent: 15 March 2005 11:47

Hi lol,
Thanks. I don't think that there are any other changes. I feel really excited yet scared. The next lot I sent are closer, the early memories are sort of about something long past the next lot are about us. For me sitting in that room was so important, but I guess for you it was tough. I know that you won't judge me on them, but a bit of me is kind of scared about putting you through it again. I think that since I've started with the (name of agency). I've seen it from the other side and know that wading in other peoples shit is bloody awful. Will you share with me, like you did in the early memories bit, how it was for you at the time. I think I need to know, even if you didn't want to be there.
Catch you later Alex

From: dalesunnyplace
Sent: 18 March 2005 09:41

Hi Alex,
Thank you for your email.

Yes, I think the next bit will be tough, and yes I will share with you what it was like for me. I don't think it will take me anywhere I am not willing to go, I feel really touched by your concern though. I haven't looked through my journals for that time yet, but my memory of those sessions is that sometimes I was "afraid" and wanted to "run", but I can't remember ever not wanting to be there. Sometimes I think that I was afraid "not to be there" because the gaps in the sessions seemed really difficult to manage.

I will be in touch soon with the next instalment.
All best wishes Sue

From: alex4research
Sent: 19 March 2005 12:24

Thanks lol – speak to you soon. Alex

From: dalesunnyplace
Sent: 19 March 2005 12:24

Hi Alex,
I attach copy of proposal[2]-waiting to hear whether it is approved.

When we spoke the other week I talked about the definitional ceremony. I have sent you via snail-mail some more information about this. You said that you would feel happy about me telling the story of our conversations about suicide to a group of "outsider witnesses". Is this something which you are still happy for me to do? Is there anything you specifically want to say?
Sue

From: dalesunnyplace
Sent: 22 March 2005 09:27

Hi Alex,
I've been typing up some notes for the middle section "mid-day". I have attached them for you to look at and amend.

Reading through them, I feel really sad. Part of me wants not to send them because they portray anguish, your anguish, and I suppose I want to protect you, you've done so much soul searching. Do you need to go there again? Yes you are allowed to say again, "for God's sake get a grip" but, I do want to remind you can withdraw from this. I would respect your decision.
Sue

---

[2] A formal proposal for my dissertation was submitted to the university for academic and ethical approval.

From: alex4research
Sent: 24 March 2005 12:24

Hi lol,
Yes I am going to say "get a grip". I guessed that it would be hard for you to type up the notes, that's why I warned you but I already read them before I sent them, and have worked through some of the stuff with (name of therapist). I will look at them over the weekend and send back.

The definitional ceremony sounds fine. I don't want to be there, but would like you to share with the group our conversations. Suicide is just such a secret thing; I need others to know how it was. Perhaps you could read them a bit perhaps the beginning bits[3].
Catch you soon. Alex

Alex: May-June 2000

Several years after she left
I was on my own.
Had been alone for so long,
everyone had given up visiting.
Wouldn't have let them in, even if they had!
Spent my days drinking trying to escape the
thoughts of them going,

I couldn't go on.
Felt like shit for so long.

Sat on the floor
thinking and planning

I can't describe the pain,
my whole body ached with it.

---

[3] The narrative referred to here is presented in chapter five.

The voices in my head taunting, screaming.
Hitting my head against the wall to
STOP THEM.
Still feeling, drinking, longing for numbness that
wouldn't come.

Scratching at my hands, biting.
Chaos ebbing away.

Years ago I was a member of the gun club.
Still had it in the lock up..

I remember keeping it there as an insurance
In case I needed to end it.

Couldn't get the fucking thing to work though
Tried to get it in my mouth with my hand on the trigger
Couldn't reach ...

O God. I can't go on with this?
Too hard to say all this.

Frustration, tears, so many fucking tears.
Arms not long enough.
Sweating straining, swearing, cursing, sweating again.
No good.

Couldn't do it.
Failed.
"Couldn't even blow his f***head off" she'll say.

"Can't get anything right".

Try again,

and again.

Curl up in the corner against the wall

exhausted.

Feel the solidness of it and feel a
sudden wave of energy.
I hurl it against the wall.

Crack.

Deafening in the silence.
Then footsteps.
Banging on the door
police appear.
Have no strength to fight
they take it away, and lock it, and me up.
Separately of course.

Can't even look at it now.
Revoked my licence.

I was good. The club said I was the best in the team.
No more. Can't even do that anymore

Failed.
FAILED.

The next time I tried I drove to a quiet spot with a bottle of
booze
and some crushed paracetemols mixed with Gin
(makes them easier to swallow).

I meant to go that night
I wasn't just being dramatic
I was calm
I wrote letters, made a will.
Just couldn't stand the pain anymore.
I listened to Led Zep on the car recorder and had taken about
half the booze and paracetemols
when I got it in my head to phone her.

Stupid git!
I drifted in and out

Peaceful, for a time peaceful.

When I came to I was vomiting over a vengeful nurse.

I tried everything,
pulling the drips out,
refusing to eat/drink.
But it was no good they were determined to keep me alive.
Punishing me for what I did.

Since then I have made about 4 serious attempts,
plus the usual driving too fast and closing my eyes.
Always chickened out though.

Sad aren't I?
Thinking about it all the time, thinking, planning..

Next time I won't fail.

Hearing of others with cancer has made me feel bad.
Why were people who want to live dying
and me who wanted to die living?

Sort of sick.

That's why I'm here.
A suicide failure.

Got to find another way.

Perhaps there is a God and he doesn't want me there?
This is Hell.

I want this shit to stop
I can't go on like this anymore.

Journal 3rd May 2000
*Really down tonight. I feel a sense of hopelessness. Not sure if it is something that I've picked up from "A" and how he feels, or my own need to believe in what I'm doing. Perhaps a bit of both. Sometimes I walk out of a session with someone and I know that it's been ok. I've been there for that individual to the best of my ability. Sometimes though I feel like I do now useless, helpless, de-skilled, and unable to allow myself to be immersed in their world with them. My inner critic says, "told you so, what is this counselling crap anyway, just give it up. What difference can **you** possibly make to another persons life when you don't actually **do** anything".*

It's harder when I'm down to re-engage with family life. I trundle home on the bus and all I can see is "A" with the gun, it replays over and over again. It's not so much the horror of the scene, but his feelings of despair, hopelessness, and shame.

> *The image stays with me as I cook supper and talk with (name) about coursework. Will my son ever feel like "A"? I want to cry but know tears will seem inappropriate. Over supper I see the real people in my life, and love them so much, but there is this distance between us filled with the pain and shit I have been wading through with others. (name) notices the gap "it's alright I won't try and talk to you until you're switched on". They are patient with me and gradually their love bridges the gap and I'm back to my normal (whatever that is) self. I bath ridding myself of the day, and relax. What am I doing to myself and them in doing this job?*
>
> *Is the cost too high?*

NO MORE.

Whatever have I done in this world
to get so much pain?
I didn't ask for the bastards
to take away my childhood.
I asked God to help me;
I have prayed, cried, pleaded.
If he is there I must have really pissed him off!

SO ALONE

I imagine a place where it is peaceful;
not heaven or anything.
Don't believe there is one.

Just not to exist would be fine.
That'll show the bastards!

Perhaps she will care when I am not there.
I imagine **her** face at my funeral,

I am lying in my coffin, the smell of the earth solid around me,

Journal 16th May 2000

Colin, my counselling supervisor asked me an interesting question in our supervision session "Why don't you just give up on him?" Not sure that I can answer that one. I certainly am not being a good person centred counsellor. I find it very hard to stay with his agenda when all he wants to do is die. But despite this, I want to stay with him. He has survived so much. All he is asking is that I listen he has made it clear he doesn't want me to "do" anything. I didn't realise how hard it would be to listen though. What is wrong with me? Why do I always get client's who want to die?

Colin laughs and says that people always find an uncanny knack of talking about things they know their listener can hear.

He sounds so smug- I feel angry!

and seeing her pain. Her crying, "if only I knew"

THAT'LL SHOW HER

I'll have the last laugh. I spend hours planning my funeral What music to have?

Who will be there?

Who will say what?

Will you be there?

I've made my will left everything;
not that there is much,
to friends of the earth.
That will make my point I think.

I think one of the scary things about moving from
thinking about dying to doing the dying, is
the pain.
Yet the pain is all I've got.
Pain is something which makes me feel alive.

If I see blood then I know I am alive,
but will there be pain in dying?
And once I'm dead what then?
Will it be oblivion or hell?
Surely it can't be worse than this hell.

Journal 21ˢᵗ May 2000
I described in supervision that the experience of working with
"A" was like that of being a "knife-thrower's assistant". I
remember years previously going to the circus with my then
young sons, and seeing an act where the scantily clad assistant
spread her arms in crucifix position against a board, whilst a
man threw daggers missing her skin by millimetres. I
remember being struck not so much by the skill of the knife-
thrower, but by the trust and belief that the woman placed in
him. If she had lost her nerve and moved, the consequences
would be dire.

Working with Alex during this time I am aware of him hurling
feelings at me in the same way the knife thrower threw the
knives. The only thing I am able to do is keep trust in him and
the counselling process.

Maintaining the relationship is **all I can do**

Living like this is hell.

Who am I kidding,
No one will care if I die.

Yes I know you say you do,
but you're not real.

You go home to your family.
Yes piss off to them,

I really mean it, they love you.
Don't spend time worrying,

I will survive.
I'm a loser, not worth anyone's worry.

Leave me alone with my fantasy.
I don't want to be here anymore.

> *Session notes 30th May 2000*
> *Not sure whether I should do something,*
> *anything? Have I made the right decision? I know*
> *"A" has rights, and as a counsellor I have*
> *encouraged him to live life in a way that finds ok,*
> *and encouraged him to believe that he is*
> *responsible for his life. I know also that the*
> *mental health teams have deemed that he does*
> *not have a "diagnosable mental illness", but it*
> *doesn't stop the panic. His life is precious to me*

Not just here
in this room,
but anywhere.

**I can't go on
like this
anymore
like someone
already dead.**

Not really living unless I'm thinking about death.
I bought a length of rope last week;

I could use it on the beam up there.

**You go on go away,
I'll hang around and wait for you to return!**

Ha – a response at last!
You hate me too don't you?

Lying in my coffin I will have the last laugh.

The rope bothers me though.
Sometimes seeing it lying there on the floor
it almost has a life of its own.
I felt really good buying it.

I imagined how it would feel as I put it round my neck,
kicked away the chair.
I felt calm in control
I practiced it in my head a few times.
It was a kind of orgasmic,

like I was
invincible.

> *Journal 5th June 2000*
> *Telephoned Colin which was something, rather than nothing. Talking it through with him helped me see what my responsibilities were what the ethical implications may be. We decided together that breaking confidentiality would not be right. I feel calmer inside, but still sad.*
>
> *Will I see him again?*

Then it became
threatening
I dream about
it sometimes

The rope
It changed to
the rope having control
When I'm dead I won't have any control will I?

It's like tiptoeing across eggshells

one slip and I lose
the plot for ever.
Yet even as I plan
dying
I do it to live,
or to survive
living.
Sometimes I
really want it to
end

> *Journal 6th June 2000*
> *How will I cope if "A" does die? I woke this morning going through what I would say to "A's" mother. What I would say to the coroner my mind re-calling bits of our conversation. could I have changed anything?*
>
> *I keep looking at the telephone, then when it rings I jump out of my skin.*

life just seems too fucking difficult.

Living, and enduring this living by imagining death.
A living hell.

Surely death would be better than that?

**They will say
poor old bugger**

**he lost it big time
failed at living.**

Perhaps that should be my epitaph:

"failed at living"

So far I've failed at dying
so I suppose that would be
different!
Don't know why I laugh,
but laughing sometimes helps.

Journal 7th June 2000
"A" telephoned, such a relief.
I feel like singing!

Sometimes when we both laugh together it feels possible.
The laughter makes it ok somehow.

Like angels wings in the dark place of my heart.

Supervision notes 15th June 2000
I couldn't wait to get there. Talked through
with Colin the roller-coaster feelings of the
preceding week. Glad that what I'm experience
is normal. Colin thinks that trusting "A's"
decision will be a turning point. I hope so, I
don't want too many more weeks like this one

Can I change?
I hope so
I want to live and
think of living
rather than dying
**How can I
escape?**

Journal 16th June 2000
Why do I not give up on him? Colin's question echoes:

Firstly I suppose it has to do with my past professional experiences of working with other people. Alex is not the first suicidal client I have worked with and I do not expect he will be the last. Staying with the chaos seems to be the only skill I have to offer in a situation where I often feel de-skilled and helpless. I go back to my person-centred roots and focus on creating a relationship.

This focus on relationship is backed up by my reading round the subject. For example Heckler (1994) undertook research with a group of people who had recovered from suicide attempts. He found that one of the things these survivors found helpful in their "return to life" was having relationship with other people. He observed the suicidal entering what he termed as a "suicidal trance" which isolated the person from others and reality. Breaking this trance through relationship helped the person to move way from suicidal behaviour. Isolation is also shown as one of the high risk factors in other quantitative studies (Pritchard 1995) so staying in relationship seems important. "Trusting the process" as my diploma tutor would have said.

I am reminded of psalm 22 "My God, My God why have you forsaken me". Christ's words expressing anguish on the cross, and the two Mary's abiding presence. To see a loved one tortured to death surely must be worse than death itself. Yet they stayed and bore witness. There is something for me of "bearing witness" that is part of me and what I do, and indeed there have been times when I have been grateful for others "bearing witness" to my pain. To walk away from Alex would be like turning my back on the cross of Christ, of never encountering Easter and the joy this brings. Turning away would be like saying to that other person "you have to bear this alone, you can only tell me things within my comfort zones". It would be different if I was referring a person to someone who was more expert in a particular area, I do have limitations of experience and skill- I recently referred someone for specialist psychosexual therapy, and that did not feel in the least like giving up on them. Walking away from Alex would be different; it would mean putting more value on what was comfortable for me, against his need, possibly his life.

My memories of a 42 year old man dying, leaving behind a family despairing. I often wonder if there would have been a different outcome if there had been someone there who could have listened to his pain. I don't give myself too hard a time about not listening then-I was a sixteen year old girl with no knowledge of what appeared obscure adult behaviours.

But I am no longer a child, but a woman who can stand alongside, and does. I have despaired of life itself, I have stood on the lonely hillside wishing I had never been born, and I have come to value life as precious, God given. I respect the courage Alex and those hooked into cycle of suicidal behaviour and their desire to change. I respect his courage at sharing (when so many others have reacted abusively and violently). Surely listening is the least I can do.

I am aware though that this kind of listening not only affects me, but it affects my family. I need to balance work with home. I do not want to lose the love of my friends and family, I need to look to their needs also.

Email Conversations about Research
April 2005

From:alex4research
Sent: 03 April 2005 09:44

Hi lol, I've been reading through the stuff you typed.

It's hard to believe I said these things. I don't know why you didn't tell me to sod off. I sound so angry. A whole lifetime of anger. I guess I was scared too, that you would say sod off like everyone else. When I grew up and met (name) I didn't have those kind of thoughts hardly at all, but when she left the whole thing exploded- all the abuse memories came back and I just was in that place again. She just said it was blackmail and left anyway. The doctors- well you know about them. They just pumped me full of mind numbing crap and told me not to talk like that.

But I needed to get it out somehow. So just having you listen was enough. amazing but terrifying. You felt powerful just sitting there. I didn't know it was so hard for you though. Seeing your journal makes it feel kind of more ok. Not sure why. Will think about it some more. Haven't made many changes.

Speak to you soon Alex

From: dalesunnyplace
Sent: 03 April 2005 12:37

Hi Alex,
Thank you for the email. I am away until Wednesday will write more then. Best wishes Sue

---

Alex: June–September 2000

I am so alone.
Everything seems totally pointless,
meaningless.
Each day something that has to be endured.
The future never ending.

I don't want to go on..

It's not (name deleted) that's just like a final straw.
I just don't want to be here.
Not anywhere..
But there's my parents,
and ..
I wonder whether I should stop seeing her (name)
That would be hard.
I couldn't

love her more if she was my own.

Then if anything happens to me, it wouldn't hurt her so much?

> *Session notes 16th June 2000*
> *I feel that I want to avoid his despair, but also know that its important to stay with him in the chaos. I feel strengthened as I look at the wall in the room which divides this building from the church next door. Something about its strength and endurance which steadies me. It's strange, "A" can seem to tell (without me saying anything) whether I can cope with what he is telling me, his desperation. I wonder whether these childhood losses are significant. I notice he is weeping silently.*

Children
get used to
people not
coming,
don't
they?..
I remember
losing
people when
I was a kid.

O God
I can't bear it,
it was so awful.

Not seeing her would be just as bad as dying wouldn't it?

I just can't bear living like
this,
every day is such hell.
Even getting out of bed is a
major test.

> *Session notes 16th June 2000*
> *Feel pressure. He wants me to say that I'll miss him. Why can't I say that? It's true I would miss him.*

What's the fucking point?

No-body would miss me.

I've written letters to all of them
Apart from my folks.
All the people I care about.
If anything happens to me now everything is in order.

I can't write to them though
I can't find the words yet.
Not for my folks.

I thought that the knives will do the trick this time,
I could cut my arm.
Just here where the main artery goes.
Look I'll mark it with pen!

Session notes 16th June 2000
I feel cold and sick. Hope that I don't
throw up. I feel very vulnerable and
exposed. I will be away next week, but
refuse to justify or defend.

Don't worry
I won't make a mess on
the rug.
I'll be here when you get
back.

I was so angry with
HER
with you,
with me, for saying what I said.

I needed her and she pissed off.
I needed you

Session notes 27th June
We talked about his reaction to me
going away last week. I agree to give
him more notice if I can.

He says that he feels embarrassed by
his reaction. We talk through what
embarrassed is like.

and you weren't here.

I felt so jealous
of your life.
You could see what I was
going through
yet you could get up and
go away.

I imagined you laughing with your family
and I hated you for being so happy.

I wanted to destroy everything.
Myself.
Her.
You.

and yet in the same moment I knew you needed a break
and I knew you would come back.

I feel so ashamed.
I do trust you,
but it's like I've showed too much of myself.
I don't like needing people.

I've said it now though.
First time face to face.
They raped me

I've finally said it.
Usually if I get too close to saying it I
go off on one – you know
self-hate, loathing.
I expect to see
contempt.

You didn't flinch though
accepted.

I expect you think it deep down.
No-one could really accept me after what I've said.

I can't believe I've been stupid enough to say it.
Although it's a kind of "yes" moment,
I'm scared of tomorrow.

Will I regret what I've said?
You will always know now
I can't take it back.

Will it come between us?

I'm scared now it's out in the open,

will it destroy me?

Will I self-destruct?

I opened the can of worms

Now I can't put them
back.
You know something on
me
I hate it.

Session notes 7ᵗʰ July 2000
"A" started by fantasising about his
funeral, how he would die, I wonder if
this is related to our conversation last
week about childhood abuse, and ask
him about it

I know in one way

I have to talk,
get it out before it
destroys me.

I'm so angry for letting it out.
Angry with you for letting me say it.
You have one on me
DYING SEEMS A GOOD ESCAPE.

Transcript of session 7ᵗʰ July 2000
"You trusted me now you wish you hadn't?"

I've never told
anyone else

I feel frightened that you could hurt me.

I'm glad I talked though,
just gets

scary

It's ok when I'm here,
but when I'm alone,
the other part of me
is so scared.

Transcript of session 7th July 2000
"You are here-you chose not to die today"

I am here.
Part of me always reacts
to being scared
by wanting to die.

Planning to die gives me back control
You understand now don't you?

But if I die, I will never understand
will I?
I need to understand.

You know—I need to
live without all these thoughts of dying.

I really do want to find another way.

I can't stop life from being crap,
from scary things happening..

But for fucks sake I am not 7 now

I am a man,

I don't have to have all these crappy thoughts.

Talking about them kind of helps though.

Do you want me to stop coming?

Session notes 28th *July 2000*
*"A" talked about his feelings of desperate loneliness. He hasn't spoken
to anyone since me last week. "I can't go on feeling like this. Life isn't
worth living if it has to be like this". He goes on to talk graphically
about the ways he can kill himself. He stresses he doesn't want this to
happen but "can't live like this".*

*It feels abusive. I want to get up and run away (or at the least put up
strong defences). It feels like he is saying "you should be doing
something- because you haven't I will kill myself". I am concerned and
ask "A" if I could speak with his GP. He refuses saying he doesn't
want him to interfere. He then reassures me that he is not going to "do
anything silly".*

If something doesn't change
I will end up dead.
If I overdose or fall drunk
no-one will notice for a week.
You'd notice if I wasn't here though?
My body wouldn't be too awful then...
Would it?

Session transcript 28th *July 2000*
"Is that what you want?"

NO
I want to live

but..
I don't know how.

How would you feel if I died?

> *Session transcript 28th July 2000*
> *"I would feel awful. I don't want you to die I believe in you, but the choice is yours. I will support you in whatever ways I can though.*

The feeling of despair is always there.

I don't know how much longer I can go on feeling like this,
I do want to try to find a better way.

Each day is torture,
life has been such a struggle.

No-one has ever said they care
whether I die or not.
Called it emotional blackmail
they just want to cover their backs!

You care though.
Thank you.

> *Journal 28th July 2000*
> *As "A" spoke of his parents never quite understanding. I felt close to tears. I want to reach out to the lonely child. I think of my own children.*

They tried–my parents
but they never quite
understood what I needed.

I wish they had let me die,
or never had me.

It's crazy saying that
because it makes me

want to live more!

Supervision notes 7th August 2000
We review my work with "A" I find working with his self-harm and suicidal talk hard because:

    a) he uses it manipulatively and at times abusively
    b) listening to his extreme pain is very hard

In encouraging him to talk about suppressed/repressed feelings I am doing what his parents didn't; allowing him to find ways of expressing his feelings. His main defence escape seems to be isolation. Switching off to escape pain by using fantasy about death.

Email received August 2000
Hi lol,
It's always been the planning to die that has kept me in control. But when it gets to doing it, acting on the thoughts and then being brought back to life it becomes real. That kind of real I don't want. I think that I need to make some kind of sense of why I need it? Am I crazy?

If I don't make sense of it I can't move forward. I'm stuck like a rat in a trap always planning to die just to get through the living.

Perhaps I was right, I am crazy!.
Catch you later. Alex

Email Conversations about Research
April 2005

From: alex4research2004
Sent: 06 April 2005 08:51

Hi lol,

I laughed a lot when I got your email. It was as if you still thought I'd have a problem with the gaps. It's strange, but reading through the stuff now I understand more about why she left, why she couldn't handle it. I think for a long time now I've come to accept that she did leave and that I could move on and make a new life, and I have. Seeing how tough it was for you to listen to me- and it was your job; when I went off on a suicidal trip I guess I understand more about how it was for her, and I forgive her more. Never thought that I'd live to say that!

I know I said I didn't want to include the conversations we had about what happened to me as a kid, but think I would like to explain a bit so people understand why I was like I was. I felt scared when I talked to you about it, hence the reaction of warning you off with all the suicidal crap. Telling you was important though, and you staying with it despite what I put you through. When (name) left[4] I was hurtled into a world that I'd thought I'd closed the door on for ever in glorious technicolour. I thought I'd go to the grave never letting on, but it was ok saying it to you because you never defined me by what had happened to me as a kid, or how I coped with it, and that means now I can be more than that shit. It is still painful, I lost my childhood and you don't recover from that. But it is just part of my life now, and I am not chained up by it now. My other life happenings are more important. I can say what I want about it without wanting to die.

I wanted you to include this, because it's the reason behind the suicidal crap, and makes sense of it.

When I was 6 through to when I was 15 I was raped, beaten, tied up, a slave to a gang of local thugs. I survived by having this fantasy place I could escape to, where I had ultimate control over my body. It was a brilliant way of coping at the time, and I'm proud of that kid for surviving. I don't need to go to that place now though which I am glad about. It was hard to say at the time but now its ok and I'm kind of proud of that too.

---

[4] Alex felt that the breakdown of a long term relationship, and his partner leaving was the key factor in triggering his suicidal thoughts and feelings

Do you think that you can include this?
Catch you later. Alex
P.s. hope you had a good break over Easter.

From: dalesunnyplace
Sent: 06 April 2005 12:18

Hi Alex,
Thank you for the email. Yes of course I will include it, and I'm glad that you are proud!
Best wishes, Sue

CHAPTER SEVEN

EVENING

Introduction

I always have ambivalent feelings about the onset of evening. In one sense it is usually a time of unwinding from a day of activity, and time with my family which is special, it is also a time when the day seems to me to be dying. I am visually impaired and have no night vision, so it is the time I prepare to lose my sight again. It is a time of grieving for a world of colour that has turned grey. It is a time to rely on other senses apart from vision. It is a time of feeling, hearing and smelling. It is as Sen writes a time of lamentation,

"I go out in the grey evening
In the air the odour of flowers and the sounds of lamentation.
I go out into the hard loneliness of the barren field of grey evening
In the air the odour of flowers and the sounds of lamentation". (Sen 2005)

The evening is a time of gathering my thoughts, thinking about my work of the day and the people I have spoken with, and preparing for the night and the new dawn that will surely follow.

This chapter explores a new phase of working with Alex, one where he is starting to look for alternative stories to live by and we are moving towards the ending of our counselling relationship. It also follows my struggles as I discover my long term supporter and mentor, my supervisor Colin is dying, and what that means to me and to Alex.

Supervision is the key to all good counselling. As Houston (1990) points out it is where as counsellors we are "enabled" (Houston 1990:1) to be the best counsellors we have it within ourselves to be. The supervisor not only acts as a gatekeeper of the profession and ensures that our practices are ethical and that we are not harming our clients, but also gives us space to take an overview of our practice. My counselling relationship with Alex was sustainable because I was held by Colin my supervisor and felt safe. When he became ill and died not only did I grieve for him, but felt isolated and abandoned in my work. As you read the next instalment of our narrative you will see how this impacted on Alex and the therapeutic encounter.

Alex: October 2000-March 2001

Keeping this journal is good
writing it all down when I get bad days
I can remember.
I can try to
figure it out.

> *Journal 28th Oct 2000*
> *Have been to see Colin today for supervision session. He is dying. Not sure how I feel? Empty, scared, sad, perhaps all three. He would like to continue as normal with our supervision sessions.*

Talking is amazing too,
thought that I'd feel
vulnerable.
I did at first,
SCARED SHITLESS!

Scared she'd take this away from me.
My secret place.

I have to have this place to go to
where I have control.
Doesn't mean I'm going to go through with it
"do anything silly" as my mum would say.
Years ago I spoke to my GP he sent me to this guy
a cpn[1] I think he was.
He said this was

WRONG THINKING
needed help.

---

[1] Community Psychiatric Nurse

They put me away,
well not away, they suggested going in to this
mental hospital place.

They talked of drugs,
therapy which would stop me thinking like this.

So scared

Journal 10th Nov 2000
Supervision session on the surface was as
normal. I'm not sure I can do this though.

Colin has been my mentor for four years, it
is he that has given me the courage to
work with clients, to trust myself. I want to
be there for him during these final weeks.
Today we spent time with him talking
about dying and his fears. It wasn't a
supervision session but it was I think
helpful to him though.

"don't take this away
from me

it's how I survive".

Next time I met him
I told him
that I wasn't thinking
like that again.

The secret was safe.

This time it's different,
she doesn't tell me I'm wrong to have this place,

I guess she secretly thinks it,
or thinks that I will give it up.

But that's up to her!

At least she's not telling me what to fucking do.

I have always had to have this door around,
I need now to give myself space to choose other routes,

Journal 1ˢᵗ Dec 2000
I wanted to phone Colin re "A", but didn't want to put more on him. I
am however very concerned for this person's safety, and he is my
supervisor. In the end I didn't phone.

How can I talk to a man who is dying, and hating it, about a man who
longs to die, and is threatening suicide. Six months ago I would have
rung knowing that we could talk through all the ethical issues and
make a collaborative decision. Perhaps I need to start looking for a
new supervisor, but even saying that seems disloyal.

---

other doors could be better
you know.

TRAPPED
is what triggers it mostly.
But trapped is something that I can explore and find
other answers.
And trapped can mean I have chosen
not to take this door any more.

I do have choices now.

Trapped is a self-imposed prison
the door is wide open now

I choose not to go in.

The sirens wail, they pull me to the rocks

God it feels good to walk past and say:
"Fuck I don't need to travel through there again".
I miss it though,
the adventure;
the secret; having a secret is power.

The adrenalin rush
God like I stand
with the power of life and death.
But I don't miss the
CRAP.
The waking up in a hospital
throwing up.

Needles and tubes jabbed haphazardly,
painfully by hard women.

Their scorn.

Their knowledge that I'm the lowest
kind of shit that ever lived.
Couldn't even succeed at that:

"Loathsome creature"

Journal 14th March 2001
Colin died yesterday.

It feels as if there is this huge gap, this emptiness that will never be filled. It was very hard to work today, I felt so very alone. I don't think that anyone really understands how I feel about losing him. "He was only your supervisor" says a friend, but it is as if he underpinned my work, especially my work with those who self-harm, his support enabled me to feel safe, work safely.

Selfishly I feel he has abandoned me.

I hate myself more than ever the nurses can.
I hate myself for trying,

even though it wasn't my choice,
I couldn't stop.

The fantasy had a life of its own.
Terrified.

Trapped.
Again out of my control.
Out of my control
again

Journal 18th March 2001
Crisis with "A" I think that he senses I
am less available to him somehow, we
had an awful session, he told me to "piss
off back to my family" Asked (name) for
a   peer   supervision   session;   she
understands my work, and I trust her
judgement. Have also made a date to
meet with a new supervisor. If I don't get
the supervision sorted, I will have to
stop working with him.

Perhaps next time will
be the last.

Even you are not here
for me now

You sit there so far
away.

Why don't you

piss off back to your family.

Just piss off.

There is just no point in being here.

PISS OFF!

Leave me alone.

Email Conversations about Research
April 2005

From: dalesunnyplace
Sent: 06 April 2005 11:34

Dear Alex,
Thank you for the email, of course it can be included, it is as you say important. I thought that I would include the whole email if that is ok with you. How we view the conversations now seems to be an important part of the story we are telling. Is there anything else you want to include about what happened to you?
Best wishes Sue

P.s. Yes, the gaps were difficult for me at the time, I was never sure if you'd be there when I got back, but without them we wouldn't have learnt to trust each other. I am still very conscious though of letting people know when I am not going to be around.

From: alex4research
Sent: 19 April 2005 09:03

Hi lol,
Thanks for the message.

I think that what I've said is ok. If we go any further down that route you'll have to write a book on abuse rather than suicide. Yes, I think it'll be good to include the emails. It's strange, talking about it with you was a first, and at the time it was kind of miraculous to just say it.

If we hadn't been able to talk I think that I'd have ended up dead if not deliberately certainly accidental.

I needed to understand why I had such crap thoughts. Talking about them with you meant that I could look for alternatives.

It's been an eye opener reading through this stuff. It's kinda of like a final goodbye to those times.

I'm glad we are writing it down. I want others to know that they can escape the crap self-destruct thoughts. I want there to be more folks able to listen to them.
Catch you later, Alex

From: dalesunnyplace
Sent: 19 April 2005 11:41

Thanks Alex. Yes I will make amendments
I get a sense from reading through the journals that it was when you were
able to understand more about the way "the suicidal thoughts" were used
by you that you were then able to find different ways of coping with the
"memories of what happened to you as a kid"–there is a sudden change in
the way you write–it is as if something has clicked into place–can you
remember anything about that? (I attach the bit of journal I mean)
All best wishes Sue

From: alex4research
Sent: 19 April 2005 18:03

Hi lol,
I've read through the bit you are talking about. Yes. I think that it was
when you asked me whether the suicidal thoughts were connected with
what I had told you about when I was a kid-something just clicked-I kind
of realised what I was doing to avoid thinking about those times. Once I
knew that I could make sense of it somehow and I could look at those
things which happened to me-if the suicidal thoughts crept in then I knew
why and they didn't trouble me so much.

Does that make sense? Alex.

Alex: March-April 2001

Transcript of session 23rd March 2001
"Are you saying you would feel better
if you moved?"

No
not really
I think I'll only
feel better..

When I rejoin the real world.

I've built this wall around me to protect me
because
I'm so scared about being hurt by other people.
Isolating myself;

keeping control by planning
how I'll die.

This keeps people away.
**Except for you of course
ha! ha!**

The real world is this though,
sharing life with others;
not just you,
with other people.

Leaving death to
fate or God.
Whatever.

> *Journal 24th March 2001*
> *I talked with "A" about what becoming real*
> *is about. I am reminded of the book called*
> *the little velveteen rabbit, "real happens to*
> *you when a child loves you for a long, long*
> *time not just to play with, but really loves*
> *you...you become". (Williams 1922:8)*

Real is about
looking at now
and being able to

change something now.

I don't need to have control over life itself.

Real would be..
Someone loving me for being me.

Guess that might not happen,
but hope that one day it will.
Where I live,
for now anyway,
is enough for me to feel
I have some control over my life.
Another positive way of escaping the

> Session notes 23rd March 2001
> Strange, a really positive session. As
> we come towards the end he starts
> talking about wanting to be dead. I
> challenge him (which at the beginning
> would have felt terrifying) and ask him
> if he doesn't want the session to end.
> We then finish with warmth and
> laughter and agree to meet next week.

TRAPPED

What I need from you
is the strength

to survive the day.

If I survive today I can
survive anything.
Sometimes the temptation to go back to that door
Is more than I can bear,
but life is all I've got,

and I'm going to live it

as long as it lasts.
That sounds like a new beginning?

Email Conversations about Research
April 2005

From: alex4research
Sent: 25 April 2005 09:01

Hi lol,
I have sent you some more journal stuff connecting with escape from the
suicidal crap.
Speak to you soon. Alex

From: dalesunnyplace
Sent: 25 April 2005 16:36

Thank you Alex.

It sounds as if making sense of the suicidal thoughts was very important in the thoughts "not troubling you so much", and when they did not trouble you so much you were able to explore the "things that had happened to you" and make sense of them. Looking through your journal there is little said about the thoughts at this time. Did they completely go, or were they still around but you did not need to mention them?
All best wishes Sue

From: alex4research
Sent: 29 April 2005 17:46

Hi lol,
At the time I couldn't think of anything but me. Dying seemed my choice and other people saying it was wrong thinking seemed to take away any respect for me and my choices and because dying was so important to me and I didn't have any other ways of coping it felt as if they were saying I was worthless. My choices were worthless. This fed into the cycle of "I don't deserve to live". The more they said you must not do this the worse I felt and the more I wanted to die. The guilt pile on me was huge.

When I see it all written down and how you felt sometimes I can understand a bit more where the medics were coming from. You were scared some of the time about what would happen to you if I died and now I can realise that if I had died you would have had to explain yourself and be judged by their standards. Talking through was the only way I could escape this crap though. I was stuck on this wheel not knowing any other way to step out of the wheel. Someone had to take my way of coping seriously. It was only then I could move away from it. You never said suicide was wrong but you also told me that you didn't want me to die. That made a difference. Someone cared.

I don't thinks the thoughts completely went, they popped up now and again, but I could say no I don't want to go there again. Now I rarely if ever have them. They were a way of coping then. Once I understood what was happening I had more choices, and I chose to live.
Does this make any sense? Alex

PART 3:

ENGAGING WITH LIFE

CHAPTER EIGHT

NIGHT

Journal 20th April 2002
I stood on the step outside the cottage and looked up with amazement.
Here in the dark still night I beheld a wonder.

The milky way exposed before me.

I had never ever seen anything like this before. It was as if the
hardness of the night had ended, yet dawn was still far off; and if you
watched carefully the whole of the heavens was connected with me and
me with them.

I was alone no more.

Introduction

When writing the narrative accounts of the conversations I had with
Alex I wanted to do more than report on a phenomenon. As Richardson
states, much social science research contains, "repetitive authorial
statements and quotations; "cleaned up" quotation, sonorous prose
rhythms; dead or dying metaphors" (Richardson 1992:30).

I wanted the stories Alex and I had written to resonate with the reader
in order that some understanding of our lived experience be conveyed, and
hopefully the narrative accounts of our conversations do provide this. It
was also important to both Alex and me for these often silenced stories to
be told in ways that broke through the silence. Having had some
experience of using "definitional ceremony" as described by White (2000)
I suggested to Alex that we could tell our stories within this kind of setting
in the hope of making the "lived experience" of our conversations
understandable and meaningful to others, and also as a way of helping us

link our experiences with others who may have had similar experiences. As Ellis and Bochner (1992) point out, "the act of telling a personal story is a way of giving voice to experiences that are shrouded in secrecy" (Ellis and Bochner 1992:79).

Definitional ceremony is a metaphor developed by cultural anthropologist Myerhoff (1982; 1986; 1979) in her work with a Jewish community living in Los Angeles. Many had lost families in the holocaust and they became increasingly elderly, isolated and invisible to the wider community. Myerhoff noticed however that they were a community who were conscious of their connected-ness with each other and their joint histories of stories, but that natural occasions for sharing these histories of stories were lacking and had to be artificially invented. She called these inventions "definitional ceremonies", which gave this group of people an opportunity to share their "collective self-definitions" (Myerhoff 1982:105) witnessed by a wider community. The re-telling of these self-definitions by the witnesses gave authentication to the identity claims of the storytellers. Joint themes were found which connected people. There was a gathering together through storytelling of all those past and present members of this joint story, connections were then made with the experiences of the witnesses in the wider community. The fragmented, and isolated, became visible and part of the wider community once more.

White (1995; 2000) was interested in using this definitional ceremony within a therapeutic setting, where people could engage in telling of stories relating to their lives, which were then witnessed by others. The telling and re-telling of stories with shared themes connected lives and provided a richer fuller sense of identity to the participants, and gave voice to often "silenced" stories, and it was my experience of this work and reference to other researchers such as Speedy (2007; 2004) which influenced my decision to use it for research.

Definitional ceremony (although differing in content and style, according to need), takes the following basic shape. Firstly the storyteller tells the story (aided by an interviewer) in this case it was the story of conversations about suicide focussing on my work with Alex. The witnesses having listened to the story in the position of an audience, then engage in re-telling what they have heard (aided by an interviewer) in terms of how this has resonated with their own life stories (the storyteller during these re-tellings is now in the position of audience). The original storyteller (aided by an interviewer) then re-tells his or her story in response to what he or she has heard in the re-tellings of the witnesses. The group then join and reflect on the process as a whole. It is in this telling and re-telling that there is a linking of lives. People are connected around shared themes, and the storyteller's story is authenticated and a new fuller sense of identity emerges. Each person is "seen in one's own terms, garnering witnesses to one's own worth, vitality and being" (Myerhoff 1986:267).

This chapter continues to tell the research narrative through email conversation and then explores the definitional ceremony which was held in May 2005.

Email conversations with Alex
May 2005

From: dalesunnyplace
Sent: 02 May 2005 10:40

Hi Alex, thank you for the email. Yes what you say makes a lot of sense, I will include these emails if I may? I have just received feedback from the external examiner on the dissertation proposal:

> **"Susan Dale** This is a well thought out research proposal that should give counsellors valuable insight into clients exploring suicidal thoughts. It has potentially great implications for training and supervision of counsellors and should add to the small but growing research work already undertaken into this area. Good ethical insights shown."

I have been typing up some more of the journal you sent to me and attach it for your amendment. It is the definitional ceremony next week, are you still happy for me to use the section Feb/April and talk about our work together?
Sue

From: alex4research
Sent: 05 May 2005 11:25

Hi lol,
The examiners comments sound good.

Yes I am still ok about the definitional ceremony and you using Feb/April stuff. Or other if you want to. **I want you to talk about it**. It would be good for others to hear how it was and is.

Let me know how it goes, Alex

From: dalesunnyplace
Sent: 13 May 2005 10:28

Hi Alex, it was so good to talk to you and tell you about the definitional ceremony. It felt to me that our stories connected with the witnesses, and that was very good.

I have sent you some more drafts via snail-mail do make amendments as usual.
All best wishes Sue.

From: alex4research
Sent: 17 May 2005 19:25

Hi lol,
It was really good to talk with you to. It feels really important that people especially among counsellors start to talk about suicide this lessens its power somehow. I have sent back some amendments. Hope that's ok

It's starting to feel as if we are coming up to another kind of ending. That feels good, and yet sad. I've got so much out of this -more than I thought. Can I read some of the stuff you write about the definitional ceremony?
Alex

From dalesunnyplace
Sent 18 May 2005 09:47

Hi Alex,
Yes, I'm transcribing the definitional ceremony, from the tape at the moment which is very slow! My intention is to use the witnesses story's within the dissertation. I want to check out with the people who shared that it is still ok for me to use their stories, and then of course I will share it with you.

Thanks for the amendments; I'm hoping to get you a draft of all the stuff we've written so far, for you to look through. Is that ok?

It's interesting that you are anticipating endings. How do you think this will feel?
All best wishes, Sue.

From: alex4research
Sent 23 May 05 12:53

Hi lol
This has been another step on my journey. Seeing my story written out has been so important. Thank you. I know that you have had reasons for writing it, but it has been another step for me in healing. I feel different, I'm proud not of the past, but I suppose of being able to live with it.

I know we probably won't speak, but I don't think I'll ever say a final goodbye. Our relationship has gone through all sorts of different phases; it's as if I don't need you as much now. You've kind of been like a mum. I know that's daft, but it's kind of like I'm ready to leave home and that's fine. It doesn't mean that I will forget you or our conversations; I just know I won't need them now.

Don't faint. (name) and I have decided to get married! I just wanted you to know.
Alex.

Definitional Ceremony May 2005

The format of the ceremony was as described in the introduction above. Alex chose not to attend in person, but with the groups permission I shared with him the witnesses' stories, and what I had written of the ceremony. He was then able to give feedback to the group by email.

I was interviewed in the presence of a group of "outsider witnesses" (White 2000). In this instance these were Doctoral and Masters students' together with university staff who were all interested in finding out more about the process of using definitional ceremonies within narrative practices, and had connections with counselling and research. The witnesses were then interviewed to re-tell parts of the story which resonated with their own experiences, and then I was re-interviewed to re-tell the story in light of the witness's responses, and then as a group we reflected on the process.

The witnesses were prepared and asked to respond to my telling of the story of Alex and my conversations about suicide, with re-tellings of certain aspects of what had been heard. White (2003) gives guidance on outsider witness responses, and these were explained to the group present.

The witnesses re-tellings were not expected to be an account of the whole of the content of what is heard by them, but those aspects of the stories that "most significantly engaged their fascination" (White 2003:3). They were asked to listen to the stories and then:

- "Identify the expression", which expression used caught the attention or struck a chord.
- "Describe the image", what image did these expressions evoke?
- "Embody the responses", what is it about your own life/work that causes these expressions to catch your attention?
- "Tell", how have you been moved or affected by witnessing these stories?

I approached the ceremony with trepidation. I was representing not just myself but also another who was putting their trust in me. I was putting our stories "out there" into the unknown, would there be any resonations with the witness's lives?

I spoke of our stories, Alex's despair, the hope of the dawn, and my struggles to hold the delicate ethical balance between "staying with Alex" and "fear of consequences and accountability".

I felt privileged to have the opportunity to speak about the unspeakable, just saying it out loud changed the story and I felt the oppressive silence lift. Listening to the witness responses I felt less alone and isolated and re-connected with a community who all had stories to tell of their experiences of connecting with suicide, the ethical dilemmas of working with the suicidal and the hope of the dawn. Although I had anticipated some resonance, I was surprised at the quantity of stories, and how these personal accounts touched me and linked our lives. My own story was re-defined by the experience.

What follows is a narrative account of the resonating themes from the witnesses. I have used the definitional ceremony participants own words, negotiating with them their format which again is in poetic stanza form. I have not, in this instance, named the participants involved as I wanted to give an impression of a "community" of stories rather than "individual accounts". I have grouped them as they emerged within five themes:

1. The dawn- a sign of hope
2. Staying with it, or walking away
3. Being close to those affected by suicide
4. Conversations about suicide in a therapeutic context
5. Conversations about suicide within the definitional ceremony.

1. The dawn: a sign of hope

"I remember sitting on the hill it was December and it was dark,
and I sat there watching the blackness.
I hadn't thought of killing myself particularly.
I hadn't got the means to do that,
but the feeling of not wanting to be there, not wanting to go on,
and not wanting to be.

I just didn't want to be.

And I sat.

As I sat the sky changed because it was the dawn.
It was such a simple thing because dawn happens every day,
but on this particular occasion
the dawn coming signified to me that
"however dark the night was dawn would come".
It felt as if God was lighting up the sky.
There was hope.

In most of the places I work now I have a picture of the dawn, not that particular dawn, but another dawn.
It is about hope.
I think in my "staying with it" there is something about knowing
that dawn will always come.
It's quite strange because after that particular dawn
I didn't do anything dramatic,
I just packed my bag and went home and got on with it, as you do."

"The thought of dawn really resonated for me in a very literal way.

From my own experience of a bad place I was in
and the light of dawn to break through the window
just gave me enough hope to go on to the next day.

And the darkness before that seemed so desolate, despondent.

With just a chink of light coming would be enough
to just go on that next small step.

In the Kipling sense "If" you can fill the unforgiving minute with
sixty seconds worth of distance from..
"holding on" gives you enough just to go that other step on."

"A strong feeling is about the dawn.
It comes to my mind the song of 'Morning has broken'[1].

Because of its huge amount of hope and reflects the hey-day of my life.
It's when you do skydive.
We should be there when dawn has come.
We have to get in the air in the blue sky.
The best time of our life, so I feel so much happier.

I think that will be my philosophy about whenever things go wrong,
there's always this."

"The word dawn resonated.
The picture of dawn that Sue keeps in different places where she
spends time.

For me it was the power of the new day emerging
and, the positive images that come with that.
They are very important to me.
I'm very appreciative of the new day.

My life has many peaks and troughs
and it's the sort of knowledge that the trough is the darkness is really
low
and that actually,
having the light physically breaking through the darkness.

---

[1] Morning has broken is a Christian hymn written by Eleanor Farjeon (1881-1965)

This powerful celestial body coming and overpowering.
The light in the world that we couldn't live without.

I am wondering whether in the same way the dawn will break
that there is a belief in Sue that how ever difficult the difficulties
they will be overcome.
But I'm not sure that's true for everyone.
For some, however dark it is the more gloom there would be."

2. Staying with it-or walking away

"You talked about all sort of things like accountability,
being scared, and so on
and you said there was also staying with it,
and this is what you did.

There were lots of other options,
like abandoning Alex,
passing him on to another person.
But you stayed with Alex.

You sat through all this
and yet despite accountability,
feeling abusive,
litigation,
being chucked out of the BACP[2]
you trusted the process.

A lot of people don't;
who work in this profession.
We read in journals
very much on the side of litigation,
accountability, be careful cover your back.
When the dawn is not enough for you, it is not enough for Alex either."

"I think that trusting the process is what keeps me there.
It gives me a tool to stay there.

---

[2] I am an accredited member of the British Association of Counselling and Psychotherapy (BACP)

I trust the process using knowledge's of other people I have worked
with,
trusting the person,
sharing contact,
relationship.

The thought of dawn in my mind which is:
Spiritual.

Dawn always comes.
There will be another dawn
every day.
However dark or hard the night dawn will always come.

And Dawn is enough.

On the other side of the balance is fear of consequences.
Once I stop trusting the process,
the stories come apart.
Once I start panicking then I cannot see the dawn."

"Something Sue said about
'that is all we can do'.

That's my own need in therapy
because I always want my therapist to do something,
to transform how I'm feeling,
but actually all that he can do is be there.
There isn't anything else.
The difference for me is
as a child you are there on your own.
I was there on my own
but with an adult visiting I'm not there on my own.
And that's all there is.

The image I've had over a long period through the process of therapy
is of a whirlpool
and I get close to this whirlpool and my therapist said to me
do you want me to keep you out of it or go in it with you.
The picture I want is of him to be in there with me."

"Sue mentioned so many times
Stay with it
It's struck me so many times about ethics.

To refer to somebody else?
Or to stay with it?
Who is the loser if you can give this client up?

The counsellor?
the client?
Although on the outside I would choose the same
I would stay with it.

Where is the boundary?
Should I go? Should I stay with it?

You have to be so careful
which is something about the limit of where I can choose to go.
I keep asking what is the limit?"

"Where is the ethical boundary?
For me this spoke of a love,
the difference between staying with the dawn and all that I could do
and the difference.

I have found myself in similar situations to Sue.
I've answered similar questions by saying
'this is all I could do' in order to actually work.

Sue spoke of a sense of responsibility towards these people
and intellectually I know too that this is someone else's problem,
but it kind of feels my own as well.

I take on board other peoples difficulties
and feel that I'm part of things,
when if you think about it in a more detached way you are not.".

3. Being Close to those affected by suicide

"It's about commitment.

A friend I had
had a brother who committed suicide
and she kept saying 'I need to be with him',
'I need to be with him'.
She showed commitment.
She was being with her family.

It was tragic, he did commit suicide.
He hung himself from the tree.

There was another brother,
she had another fear.

She had to be with him.

My commitment was to allow her to be away
while at the same time I was angry (secretly).

I was on the periphery.
I didn't know the family.
She was the one who was committed and staying with it.
My staying with it was from a distance."

"Sue was speaking about Alex
and his threats to hang himself from the beam etc.

I felt really angry
and I was imagining if that had been me.
If I'd been in Sue's position.
The threats felt really persecutory
and I was imagining how I would handle that.
I started to imagine what from my way of looking at things
what Alex was doing to her,
how he was relating to his mother,
and I started to think of my own mother who used to threaten suicide
and it was a sort of constant way of keeping me in order
I think now.

So in order to avoid that,
I would have to hold myself back.
Not be a pressure or a fuss;

and how angry that made me feel!
and that brought me back
to the anger I felt when Sue was sharing that.

The emotion and the level of anger I feel is very powerful,
so that tells me it is very powerful."

"I thought of a friend at school whose father committed suicide,
and how the family was kind of ostracised with the rest of the town I was
in.

I felt a close affinity with him in many ways.
We went to extra writing classes for our handwriting was so bad.
I met him later in life.
He had a very high I.Q. apparently
and he had become a welder in the docks and was
very unfulfilled in his life.

I heard a few weeks after we had met again many years on
that he'd committed suicide.

I liked him and his dad.
Quite an isolated family.
I felt quite an affinity with him,
a lot of people didn't,
and later in life because of my own isolation and desperation
it was something to refer back to,
that I cared the same."

"I was pitched back to another story that happened about
25 years ago.
A young man's suicide.
I knew the family very well.

He killed himself, and the family rang me up.
I know them,
they treat me like part of the family.
This was devastating for them.

When I had the phone call I felt nothing,
but as soon as I arrived there it really hit me.

I could feel the same as the family.

I stayed with them for a week and shared with it."

4. Conversations about suicide in a therapeutic context

"So you get tempted to the preferred position 'in there'
but sometimes you sit on the 'fringes',
that's quite interesting.

That's an interesting space isn't it,
between the 'fringes' and 'in there?'"

> *"Alex used suicide,*
> *and the thoughts of suicide to gain control over his life*
> *when he felt "trapped".*
>
> *I have heard it said lots of times,*
> *by others,*
> *that these thoughts and plans are helpful,*
> *even if there is not any intention of acting them out."*

"Thinking about one suicidal client
and he had attempted suicide on lots of occasions
he always wanted to walk under a train
so he would be on the train tracks,
and Sue mentioned the vivid images that she had about the shotgun
and I connected with the vivid images of him
and I would in some strange situations
washing up or whatever...
all of a sudden I would feel the impact of a train hit me.

When I worked with him that happened a lot
and it was the question of 'what are we doing to ourselves?'
What's the vicarious trauma involved in this sort of work?

I used to imagine
that this guy would be on the front page of the paper.
He would finally do it and in some way I'd be implicated.
I'd have to be at the inquest."

"The act itself is a very disconnecting act,
but the act of collectively talking about it
is a very connected act
so it's almost an opposite position.
Polarity really."

"Listening to others on a rollercoaster of emotions
has shaken me in a physical way.

Listening to somebody waving on that sea of emotion,
particularly self-harm.

One minute it's been like, a calm
almost beyond stillness,
the next moment unbearable energy that has to be released.
I think:
Get grounded."

"What struck me was the idea of a fear,
because I could really connect with that fear of what's happening to
them,
but also the fear of consequences,
personally and professionally.

I've had all those pictures and stories
that I've run through my head so many times
you know my notes being scrutinized and the..

What's intriguing me is
that there are people, who are actively suicidal,
but also the idea of people talking, thinking about suicide
in the normal course of everyday life,
and that how I think that a lot of people I've actually spoken to
and had very deep personal conversations with
have these as a really common thought
that comes to people at various times,
but that doesn't get spoken about ever and how,
I don't know,
I'm just very intrigued by this idea about this thinking,
being talked about not necessarily with any intention or any of that,
but that the thoughts come and go and how that is.

I just got very curious of that."

5. Conversations about suicide within the definitional ceremony

"What would it be like for the family in the village,
for my family,
Alex,
If there were more collective actions around this.

Those silences around it are contrary to what we're saying.
I don't know how you do it really"

> *"I feel less isolated, re-connected.*
> *Suicide is such an isolating taboo subject.*
> *I think the feeling I have now is less isolated.*
> *Working with Alex and other people has been very isolating at times,*
> *and the stories' coming from the witnesses here connects me.*
> *I feel connected to them and that is good.*
>
> *I am left asking*
> *where do you refer people on to?*
> *When you are working specifically with them*
> *on their suicidal and self-harming thoughts?*
>
> *When are they considered at risk?*
> *When they are at risk all the time.*
> *Should we be erring on the side of covering our backs?*
> *Or staying with this person in their need?*
>
> *These days I tend to work collaboratively because it makes me less*
> *isolated, and the other person is more objective.*
> *I'm immersed*
> *but someone standing on the fringes gets a better view."*

"I was afraid of this being a very heavy duty issue,
something very difficult and somehow it has great lightness.
You know these threads keep coming and going.
When Sue asked me to witness I thought I was going to be a judge or
something. It's strange to realise how many knowledge's we have of
suicide

and how much they related.

These are personal stories that have a very collective theme
everyone had related so they connect in a sense.

It is also an issue of the living.
This I start to realise,
we're all alive, talking about death, about suicide.
So in a sense we're connected with a thing that only the living can talk
about, death.
That puts a different perspective on it
because we speak about something very dark and very difficult
this is silence,
but it is only vibrant live people who are talking about this.
So I should encourage this about talking about death
and having people alive talking about it."

> *"Just thinking how engaging and positive to hear about stuff that's*
> *real.*
> *Things, generally speaking,*
> *wouldn't associate that as the right emotion*
> *to associate with such hard harrowing stories,*
> *there is a kind of quality I've been privileged to be involved in*
> *the edge of experience in peoples lives."*

"I learnt a lot, and I get the feeling I got a lot out of it as well."

> *"I got the sense that we all know several stories*
> *about how lives have been affected by suicide,*
> *you know, very directly or in passing."*

"I thought that there were a real richness of stories
and how it touches everyone's lives
and no-one really speaks about it.
They are there, but not talked about.
And touches everybody."

My initial feeling directly after the definitional ceremony was one of
relief. I felt less isolated and re-connected with others whose own stories
resonated with my own.

My next task was to transcribe the conversations and reflect further on what was said. I became more aware of how my own personal and professional stories were connected with the way in which I worked with Alex; how the metaphor of the new dawn always coming helped me stay with the dark despair, and that "staying with it" however difficult is something I value. I also recognised how important the fragile ethical balance is, especially when working with this particular client group.

This balance between the ethical guidelines the profession has adopted to protect clients against malpractice (and to protect counsellors against litigation) and the needs of the client[3], which is sometimes for us to "stay with" their despairing and suicidal thoughts. This "staying with it" is something that Alex and others value. The profession however seem to put greater weight on protecting the counsellor from complaint or litigation in the case of a client committing suicide. As Reeves and Seber (2004) point out "the fear of litigation and of 'getting it wrong' can be very powerful" (Reeves and Seber 2004:50) and get in the way of making ethical decisions based on each individual's wellbeing.

Email conversations with Alex
June 2005

Alex4research
Sent: 08 June 2005 11:58

Hi lol,
How amazing, I can't get over the stories which came out of the telling of our tale. I have just read and read them. It is so good that these things are being talked about. There is so much silence around suicide, and that adds to the problem.

Thank all the people who took part for me.
Regards Alex

---

[3] See chapter two for full discussion

CHAPTER NINE

THE RESEARCHER'S STORY

Dear Diary

Myself

September 8th 1969

I am called Susie or Sue but my real name is Susan. My age is 10 years I live at the Ambulance Houses. I have a very interesting life for my father is an ambulance driver and he gets calls from people who are trying to stay alive. My hair is hazel and my eyes are dark brown. I am tall and thin. When I have spare time I ride my byke with Franky. In the summer I like playing tennis. I only have one pet his name is Peppy he is a cat and a very naughty one at that. He eat our goldfish and left the weed over mum's chair.

I like writing stories but my teacher Mr Bumpstead says that my speling is bad. When I'm grown up I want to be a story writer like Enid Blyton and Mr Bumpstead says that is quite interesting. My Dad says that I should be a nurse and save peoples lives because that is more important than fairy stories. Perhaps I'll be a ballet dancer though as they don't need to spell, because although I would like to help people I don't like blod very much.

Introduction

When does my researcher's story start I wonder? Certainly I did not train as a counsellor with the thought of an academic or research career. I trained because I thought it was a practical skill that would help me listen to others more effectively.

My counselling tutors were truly inspirational and very supportive of my academic efforts. They encouraged me to become a competent counsellor, to look at the literature and theory surrounding counselling and to relate this to practice and my own life experiences. They also encouraged me to write, and to express myself.

Applying to do a masters degree with Bristol University seemed a huge step, and I was amazed when they accepted me, after all I had left school at 16 and had not achieved A'levels let alone a degree. Once I had got over the shock of being accepted I discovered a new world, a new way of communicating and being with people, and better ways to work with those who consulted me. The Open University has the motto "learn and live" and although not studying with the OU this is a sentiment that really resonates.

I am still not very interested in academic attainment, although I now have a doctorate, and am proud and amused, in equal measure, to prove that an ordinary woman who is visually impaired and who was told at school, "you are not really academic" can gain this kind of award. I'm not sure that I would be as interested in research or the academic in its own right, but when I link it with counselling and use it as a medium for enabling others then it becomes a passion.

What I am interested in is people. My work as a counsellor has given me the great privilege of listening to the stories of many different people from all sorts of different backgrounds. My work as a researcher and writer enables me to stand beside others who feel marginalised and without a voice to find ways of communicating to wider audiences in ways that they find empowering, and which gives them a voice which is listened to. I consider that research and writing give me a tool through which the taken for granted assumptions of society can be challenged.

Since a young age I have been a compulsive diarist and have kept a journal of my thoughts and feelings about all aspects of my life. Throughout this book you will have found excerpts from my journal which have been included to give you a flavour of my life experiences. Within this chapter I have included the journal entries made as I started to engage with research process. I then conclude the chapter with my reflections, now, at the end of this process.

Journal November 2004-April 2005

Journal October 25ᵗʰ 2004
I have just returned from my first module introducing the research unit at Bristol and don't think that I can do this.

Writing about what I do is one thing. Learning all these theories is something completely different. What is the point?

I have finished all the modules[1], and they were fine because they were about counselling and seemed very relevant to what I am doing work wise, but do I really need to know about "grounded theory" or collecting statistics and referencing? I just don't know whether this is something I want to invest time and energy in? I do not know whether "research" is for me. If I am going to do it then it has to fit in with how I work as a counsellor and make a difference to the people I work with.

Journal November 18ᵗʰ 2004
I have been looking at some of the readings for "narrative research" today which has captured my imagination. There are so many theories though, and different takes on it. At least I can read some of the articles without falling asleep! Sometimes I find something that seems to be coming from the same kind of place as narrative therapy, but there is something very slippery about trying to tie them together and; so much reading. Have just had Zoom Text put on the computer which is software that magnifies and also when needed speaks the text to me which helps my poor eyes!

I need to say who I would like my academic supervisor to be. How do I choose? Think I will go with someone that I know, and that is a counsellor first and academic second.

Journal November 20ᵗʰ
If I could somehow do a project like some kind of "case study" then that might be ok.
Some people in our group are really into analysing statistics, they really scare me. I have also met a couple of other people who are interested in

---

[1] The MSc course comprised of eight taught modules on various aspects of counselling, then concluded with a research project and dissertation

narrative research so perhaps it might be possible, we could support each other.

Journal December 1ˢᵗ 2004
I have been trying to think of something other than suicide to write about. I did write a small dissertation at the end of my diploma about working with suicidal clients and this is still something that I am really curious about. It was tough going though, writing about suicide. It made me want to give up the will to go on (just kidding!). Surely I could write about something that was refreshing and creative?

Journal December 3ʳᵈ 2004
Have been thinking about the dissertation some more, and have been talking to Jan (counselling supervisor). Whether I write about suicidal clients or not they are all around me, and I do need to work out what is going on in these relationships so that I can continue with this kind of work. Or I suppose I could just give up and do something less stressful?

There is an ex-client that I wrote something with as part of the modular course last year and I have been wondering whether he would be interested in doing a project with me.

Should I contact him though?

Journal December 10ᵗʰ 2004
Had an email from the ex-client I have been thinking about and have responded by telling him about my dissertation and asking him if he would like to be involved. As soon as I pressed the "send" button I regretted it.

What am I doing?

As a counsellor am I behaving ethically?

Journal 20ᵗʰ December 2004
Spoke with Alex (he has decided that he will stick with this pseudonym) and he seemed really excited about the possibilities of writing something about our counselling sessions. He is training as a counsellor at the moment and working as a volunteer for the Samaritans.
I am beginning to feel quite excited! But also a bit daunted. Can I do this?

I went to talk to Tim[2] about whether he would be my supervisor. I asked him because he seems the least scary of all the tutors, and when he marked one of my essays on the modular course he told me he thought that I could write. He also has an interest in counselling (and research) ethics which I think I'm going to need some help with.

Journal 23rd December
To my amazement Tim has agreed!

Journal 8th January 2005
The start of another year. I am in the process of writing an essay about the methodology proposed for my research project, and actually I'm quite enjoying the challenge. Perhaps this research is not too bad after all.

I have also received a package from Alex inside lots of notebooks containing his journal, also three tapes with our conversations from four years ago. I can't yet bring myself to read them yet, or listen to the tapes. When I start it means that there is no going back.

Rather like jumping off a diving board it will be sink or swim!

Where am I Now?

Turning this study into a book has meant reading through all of the stories again and I laughed when I came across the journal entries shown above. I have come on such an amazing journey, and I am very glad that I jumped in!

Although I meet people every day of my working life who talk to me about suicide (the statistical data I collect for the agencies I work for using CORE[3] show that 85% of my clients over the last decade have been considered to be at a moderate or high level of risk from suicide or self harm) not many of them would wish to be involved with me in writing about their experiences. As far as I am aware most of my clients go on to

---

[2] Professor Tim Bond agreed to supervise my MSc dissertation, and also supervised my doctoral study.
[3] The CORE System is for managers and practitioners working in counselling and psychological therapy services. It provides a framework for responding to the increasing demand in health and other sectors to provide evidence of service quality and effectiveness for more information see www.coreiems.co.uk

live fulfilling lives, and suicidal thoughts and feelings subside as they engage with different ways of living.

Being able to reflect with Alex over such a long period has been a privilege and given me hope. I believe it has enabled me to engage with my work more effectively. I have learnt to trust the process and the person I am working with, to stay with them as they explore even suicidal thoughts and feelings. I understand that often thoughts of suicide are the ultimate control a person has over life, so trying to stop them having such thoughts is futile and engenders much resistance and often results in the thoughts turning into behaviours. As I have stated before, if someone is talking about suicide they are not acting on it. As a great believer in life I hope that engaging people in talking about richer thicker descriptions of their lives exposes alternative stories that they can live by.

I have also learnt the value of supervision, and I never work with people who are actively suicidal in isolation. I will only work in these situations if the person gives permission to work in collaboration with their GP or mental health practitioner. Collaboration is not always easy because often medical practitioners have a different way of thinking about suicide and self-harm, but ultimately if we as counsellors are going to work in this arena we have to acknowledge the expertise of people from different disciplines and have conversations which break down the barriers.

I have learnt also that research can be therapeutic, and counselling can be research. Maintaining ethical mindfulness is of paramount importance.

So, am I an academic and a researcher?

Yes. I think finally I have shaken off the reports from my school days of "Susan tries hard but is not really academic". I see research as a way of engaging people in debate, people perhaps who traditionally do not have a voice or the opportunity to be listened to, and through this voice influencing policies which govern counselling, and mental health. I will never (well perhaps never is a very negative word) be a researcher who tries to find objective "truth" about people or situations, but I will always be committed to subjectively constructing knowledge through relationship and the stories we tell of our lives.

CHAPTER TEN

ENDINGS AND NEW BEGINNINGS

Introduction

At the end of the dissertation on which this book is based I wrote, "I am not sure whether this final chapter is the beginning of the end or the end of the beginning". The project seemed to have a life of its own, and it was very difficult to end. This final chapter of the book gives a firmer ending, but also a few tentative beginnings. I am still left with many questions unanswered.

Firstly Alex and I reflect on the research process using a narrative constructed from email conversations in 2006 (soon after the study was completed). Then I consider how the research process has affected my work as a counsellor, and finally offer some questions regarding how suicide prevention strategies can be developed in ways that promote autonomy and encourage people to have as Alex would say "a desire for life".

Email Conversations with Alex
February-March 2006

From: alex4research
Sent: 19 Feb 2006 09:28

Hi lol,
It was good to have a natter.
It's been good to have had a rest from all that thinking and reading etc.,etc., but I'm up for some more now. I think that it would be good to go back and think on how it was. Let me know how you think it would work.
Regards Alex

From: dalesunnyplace
Sent:20 Feb 2006 10:46

Dear Alex,
It was good to talk with you too.
For me I think it would be very helpful to reflect on the project to check out whether we achieved what we set out to do, and perhaps which were the most striking bits about our conversations.

We could perhaps use Email conversation?

What do you think? Sue

From: alex4research
Sent: 20 Feb 2006 17:33

Hi lol,
Yes email is great. I can reply when I have time. Talking on the phone is great but more difficult to arrange.

I suppose one of the things that stand out for me still is seeing that first story. It's like counselling changed things, but this writing it down was like moving into a different universe.

Is that the kind of thing? Alex

From: dalesunnyplace
Sent: 21 Feb 2006 08:46

Dear Alex,
Yes I think that is the kind of thing, plus what the process of doing all that "reading and correcting" was like.
How would you feel about writing something about the stories, and how counselling, and then writing it down changed things- and sending it to me?

Perhaps I could write something and send it to you- then we could see how to use it.
All best wishes Sue

From: alex4research
Sent: 23 Feb 2006 05:21

Hi lol,
Yes. I would like to do that. Sort of reflect over "that kid", and how the stories helped him.

Can I be honest? Or would you like the sanitised version? I think it would be cool if you wrote at the same time-I'd like to know what you think rather than just your response to my emails!!
Alex

From: dalesunnyplace
Sent:23 Feb 2006 08:21

Dear Alex,
Be honest of course!!
I like the idea of reflecting. It reminds me of standing by a lake in the mountains and skimming pebbles over the surface watching how the ripples affect what I can see there. Reflecting over "that kid" would be like holding him in the centre whilst we talk. Does that make sense?

Shall we go for it? Sue

From: alex4research
Sent: 23 Feb 2006 17:22

Hi lol,
Yes. Lets go for it. Alex

From: alex4research
Sent: 1 Mar 2006 21:32

Hi lol,
The first time you sent me the stuff with my own words on I cried. Seeing those words captured in a poem; so beautiful, yet telling the story of this young kid, me. I wanted to reach out and lift him from that chair. I know we'd talked about it, that was a "first" for me, sitting in that room saying those things to you. The tears in your eyes, your caring about that kid. Holding him, giving him some respect – something I'd never done.

Writing it down, keeping a journal was the next thing, and that was different again, it was a kind of promise to myself that I wouldn't forget him. I'd disowned him for such a long time. He was a past I shut away, writing in that scrappy book was a kind of promise that I knew he was there. I still didn't like him much, but he was there.

When the email came I looked at it for a bit without opening the attachment. Don't know why but it felt hard. As if I was starting something I couldn't back out of.

It took me back when I saw it. To start with I was shocked. I expected you to totally re-write my words in some kind of proper writing. Some kind of professional opinion. You know like the stuff you read in books and libraries "this guy was a 'nutter' because of what happened to him as a kid, and his relationship with his mum..etc..etc…" I know I said to you I wanted to tell my story in my own words but I didn't believe it would really be ok to do it. I thought that as this was for your course that you would want to clean it all up.

I was also curious, really curious, about how you saw me, and always wanted you to tell me what to do and how to lose that kid, but also curious to know what you thought. You were so bloody infuriating never telling me how to lose him, yet at the same time was amazing to be heard and scary all at the same time. I had times when I gave myself a really hard time about needing to talk to you, I saw it as being a wimp no man should need to talk.

Anyway back to the poem. Seeing it there, my words, God it's hard to describe. Just so fucking beautiful.

I just sat and read it. Then read it again. I wanted to put a frame round it and put it up there on the wall. This was me. I could be proud of me.

When I got over the shock and I looked at it again then I saw your words that you'd written about that kid and I felt I loved you and hated you all in the same breath. I loved you for caring for him. For being there for him and I hated you for writing these things about me that I didn't know about. That felt like betrayal. Somehow I guess I thought that my story that I told in that room was private to me. I hadn't realised that telling it to someone else would affect them too. And that they would write about it. I had a therapy session with (name) the following day and insisted that he show me any notes he took. He was quite taken aback. I need to know if people are writing about me. I felt let down. You should have told me at the time and shared what you'd written.

Now seeing the whole thing. The whole book. Knowing it has passed, that you have gained a degree from it, it has felt like my success to. My story is **good enough**. I know there will always be those who do not understand and judge me by what I did and they are not important. It's the risk you take when you put your stuff out there for everyone to see. But there might be one or two who say "yes that's something like I experience it, and if he can say it then I can say it too".

You asked me once whether I wanted to write all this in my own name and I can categorically say **No**. I could never write this in my own name it would put too much pressure on my family and me. I love writing as Alex and being "not known about". It gives me a power like I've never had before, and I can keep control. These examiner guys could meet me in the street and not know me. I trust you about that. Sorry lol, you'll have to carry the can I guess. Alex can say these things because he's Alex and not me. He is part of me, but I'm much more than him.

Seeing all these tales in print was a revelation. I could see how our sessions changed from me telling you what had happened to that kid, to a battle between me and you. An epic (Lord of the Rings eat your heart out). I was scared and in that "trapped" place where you "had one on me". I used suicide as a way of getting the control back and I threw every thing I had at you. Most people, when I was like this, walked away mighty fast. You stayed though which is why I managed to get out of the shit – the printed version told your story as well and how hard it was for you to stay, and now I finally understood more about why (name) left me.

It's like the writing down of it in the research was the next stage of therapy on from the counselling. Different, yet so powerful. Each time I tell the stories they change and becomes less powerful in the "hurting" but more powerful in the "understanding" and I hope that they give hope to others currently wading through the shit and wanting to die.

Is that enough? Regards Alex

From: dalesunnyplace
Sent: 2 Mar 2006 18:21

Dear Alex
That's quite a lot? Is there anything else?
Sue

From: alex4research
Sent: 2 Mar 2006 21:39

Hi lol,
That's about it for me I think, apart from a few comments, which might not
be printable!!

My feelings of being swamped at times by emails and words, and the
wanting to say to you (which I think I did from time to time) "for fucks
sake just write it for me". This feeling of being swamped was overtaken
though by being respected and valued and the power of being allowed to
apply the red pen. I don't think it is for the faint hearted though. It takes a
lot of time and you've got to really believe that this is something you want
to talk about. Not as simple as filling in a questionnaire!!

What was it like for you sifting through the stuff and making sense of it?
Alex

From: dalesunnyplace
Sent: 3 Mar 2006 14:27

Dear Alex,
There was a lot of fear for me. It took me ages to start and you got quite
cross with me. I remember "get a grip" you said in your email "I'm doing
this study for my reasons and you are not responsible for me".

Your words were so precious. If I trod on them, broke them in any way
with my clumsy researcher boots then I was frightened of harming you, of
offending you, of undoing anything useful that our counselling relationship
had done. Of taking you back somewhere that would be too painful.

I saw this poem, the first to emerge, and I kept it without sending it for a
few days. So fearful that despite these being your words they wouldn't be
what you wanted to say. Then I sent it and waited. The time seemed to go
past so slowly. Then your email came. I was so relieved. It was ok. We had
started and once we had started and I had added your corrections it was
fine.

Every time I sent you something my heart was in my mouth. Had I got it
right? How would you feel about what I had written?

For a time it was as if I couldn't stop writing. I had the paper by the bed
and would often jot things down as they came to me in the night (not that I
could read them the next morning?)

Sending you a copy of the whole thing was quite daunting. Although I had affirmation from my tutor that it was ok, and then knew it had passed, he was an academic, looking at it from a point of whether the methodology stood up, whether it was a "useful" piece of research, which could inform the profession. I wanted it to serve your purpose also. Had it done enough for you? Had my goal of gaining an MSc taken precedence over your needs?

Using research participants "own words" does not necessarily mean that those words convey the meaning that they had at the time of writing or saying. Language, it seems to me, conveys meaning when it is situated in context and relationship with others. As a researcher I was aware of the tension between telling your story and my purpose of reporting the experience and situating it in the context of a research paper, whose purpose was more than just "telling another's story". It needed to demonstrate academic prowess, knowledge of research and counselling theory. I tried throughout the research to make both process and content transparent and include you in the decision-making. I hope I got it right, or right enough.

Writing, it seems to me, is a different reality to the spoken word it represents. My writing about the counselling sessions was a different story from the story of "you and me speaking" in the moment in the counselling room. Within the spoken conversation our stories touched. My writing down these transitory moments in my journal and within session notes changed the story to one that you were excluded from. I wondered how you would feel seeing my counselling notes and journals. Indeed your writing contained in your journal was again not a record of our joint story, but a different story told out in your handwriting at that moment.

There were many learning's I took from this research. Learning's about suicidal thoughts and behaviours as a response to extreme emotional pain, learning's about counselling and the ethical dilemmas posed to practitioners when faced with a client who wants to explore stories of suicide, and learning's about myself as someone who has also despaired and not wanted to live.

I deliberately situated myself within the research as a participant (which was not a very comfortable place to be), but imperative if I wanted to explore the experience of our conversations and how our stories impacted on the other.

At the time of our sessions I was torn between valuing and respecting your response to extreme pain- the suicidal thoughts and behaviours kept you feeling in control and escaping the "trapped", and it was a brilliant way for that kid to cope with all that happened to him- and the dominant discourse of the society in which we live which says to us that "life is precious and must be preserved at all costs" and which influences professional ethics and governance and is often treated as a non-negotiable moral code.

As I started to see the stories emerging on the page as part of the narrative I became more aware of a battle emerging within myself between "staying with you" and the fear of "what will happen to me if you die?". My intuition told me to stay with it because this is what you needed of me, however tough the going, and I guess from what you have said this was the right decision, but would I still be saying this if you had died? I guess it's the kind of dilemma that all counsellors face at times when working with suicidal clients. Our training tells us to "stay with the client and the clients agenda" (Egan 1990 :61) but the pressure within the communities we work is that life must be preserved at all costs, and that as professionals within a litigious society we must cover our backs. If we make the wrong choices then someone may die and we may be blamed.

Understanding more about this battle has influenced my practice and my "staying with" a client is now an informed decision rather than an intuitive leap. It has also affected how I provide supervision to other counsellors who are working with suicidal clients. I am more confident in asking people about suicidal thoughts and feelings, and to my amazement many of the people I talk to are able to tell stories of wanting to die, or being close to someone who has died, and also transforming stories of coping.

Best wishes, Sue

From: alex4research
Sent: 05 Mar 2006 03:45

Hi lol,
Again what I see written has blown me away. Not quite so swampy this time but hard to let go of!

But, **I am alive** and telling these tales.

That kid is ok. I am glad he was there and part of this story to. He is part of me. I know that life is crap sometimes, **but it is all there is**.
Catch you later Alex

Personal and professional learning from the research

The main aim of this research project was to inform my own practice, and to find out "what was going on" in these conversations. I was not only the researcher, but also a research participant. To summarise, I consider the main areas of learning from this study are:

- The importance of being able to create settings where suicide and self-harming thoughts can be talked about non judgementally and respected as valid responses to emotional pain.

- How emotionally challenging it is for those doing the listening, and how isolating it can be (this was highlighted when my previously supportive supervisor became ill and died) and how important self-awareness and recognition of our emotional response and limitations are as we work alongside suicidal clients.

- The importance of developing collaborative working relationships with others, this could include working within a multi agency team, or in conjunction with a client's GP or mental health practitioner so that ethical decision making is shared.

- How vitally important it is to provide more training and support for counsellors and supervisors so they are better prepared and informed when working with suicidal clients.

- How isolating it is to have suicidal thoughts within communities who consider their aim is to "protect life at all costs", and how this isolation enables the thoughts to remain undisclosed. Spandler makes the point that repeated suicide attempts are often seen by the Mental Health professionals as symptoms of a "chronic personality disorder" (Spandler 2003:13) and that once a diagnosis is made further investigation into the causes of these behaviour ceases (Tantam and Whittaker 1992).

The National Suicide Prevention Strategy for England (DOH 2002) has stated as one of its goals to "reduce the number of suicides by people who are currently or have recently been in contact with mental health services". It has listed a number of strategies to achieve this, interestingly not including the use of counselling or any of the talking therapies, but has emphasised the need for assertive outreach teams to prevent loss of contact with vulnerable and high risk patients and also follow up for patients discharged with "severe mental illness or a history of self-harm" (DOH 2002:18). A review of the outcomes of this strategy is due at the end of 2010. It will be interesting to see whether they have been effective.

Certainly from a personal perspective it seems to have had little effect on people I work with who are diagnosed with a "personality disorder" rather than a treatable mental health illness such as depression or schizophrenia. Even if a mental heath disorder is diagnosed thoughts of suicide are often seen as a symptom of the illness to be stopped rather than explored. Alex's experience of the mental health services was one where he perceived as having "wrong thinking" and of "emotionally blackmailing" them. This, he felt, strengthened the impact of the suicidal thoughts. When writing the narrative accounts I was struck forcefully by how Alex had moved forward and engaged life when he started to privilege alternative stories to the suicidal ones, but that this only happened when he was give space and time to explore the suicidal stories fully.

The young people involved in both the studies of O'Neale (2004) and Spandler (2003) comment that for them self-harm and thought of suicide were helpful in managing their overwhelming feelings, "to myself for myself" (Spandler 2003:116). Alex talks of how as a child it was a "brilliant way of escaping and gaining control". It was only when he was enabled to explore his suicidal thoughts and behaviours that he was able to find alternative stories to live by.

Listening to the witnesses at the definitional ceremony I became aware of how many lives have been touched by suicide and despair, and how many stories are waiting to be told, but currently not being spoken, and that thoughts of suicide for some is a "way of coping". As Etherington recollects "thoughts of suicide were for many years a constant companion.....those thoughts were a kind of final solution" (Etherington 2003:186). Or as my supervisor pointed out to me within a tutorial "suicidal possibilities/vision are a way of protecting the 'survival of self' or 'personal integrity'-a source of survival and resilience".

Suicide prevention strategies which promote autonomy?

I do not think that there are many people who would dispute the need to reduce the number of deaths caused by suicide. As the Minister of State for Health pointed out in the forward to the 2002 National Suicide Strategy for England, "on average, a person dies every two hours in England as a result of suicide" (DOH 2002:3), the rate amongst young men is especially high. The English strategy (and indeed the strategies for Wales, Scotland and Northern Ireland) have responded to research in order to reduce risk in high risk groups, to promote mental well-being in the wider population, to reduce the availability and lethality of suicide methods, to improve the reporting of suicidal behaviour in the media, to promote research on suicide and suicide prevention and to improve monitoring of progress.

The strategies highlight a need for action, which is excellent, what action is taken and how it is implemented however is much more debatable.

I wanted to conclude this book by offering some questions that I hope will give both myself and the reader opportunity to reflect on how we engage with these issues. I do not have any trite answers, but hope that the questions will engage others in conversation about research and also in thinking about policies for suicide prevention and how counselling may fit in.

Firstly in general terms:

- Research shows that counselling and psychotherapy can be effective in the prevention of suicide (Winter et al. 2009) so why is it not recommended or funded?

- The UK suicide prevention strategies rely heavily on stopping people having the opportunity or means to kill themselves especially within the groups felt most at risk. Does this encourage autonomy? Does it encourage mental health professionals to ask people, "why do you feel suicide is the only solution?"

- Is there evidence that telling people suicidal thoughts are, "wrong thinking" effective in suicide prevention?

- Does preventing people from having the means to kill themselves (such as reducing the amount of paracetemols available from high street chemists) reduce suicidal thoughts and feelings?

- Most research in the field of suicide and self harm is conducted by experts talking about those who are suicidal. Is it important for research also to be undertaken by those who have experienced suicidal thoughts feelings and behaviours?

Secondly, for those of us working as counsellors with people who are suicidal:

- If we as counsellors are committed to client autonomy how do we feel about our clients having the right to end their lives if they so wish?

- Are counsellors supported sufficiently in working with suicidal clients by their professional bodies (such as BACP), and through training and supervision?

- There has been ongoing interest in secondary traumatisation of professionals working in the fields of abuse. Etherington comments of her experience of conducting research with men who had been sexually abused "listening to 25 men's stories had left me feeling overwhelmed and, I believe, suffering a degree of secondary post-traumatic stress" (Etherington 2000:145). Is this something that should be considered when working with suicidal clients? When a client vividly describes suicide attempts (or as in the case of Alex) threatens suicide the impact can be immense. I had intrusive images of Alex hanging from the beams for many months, as did my colleague who shared the counselling room and supervision sessions with me. Without the support of supervision this secondary post-traumatic stress could have been damaging.

The last word goes to Alex

I have found a way out
I never thought the shit would stop.
I expected, craved oblivion.
My way of coping with all the crap in my head
was to plan dying.
I escaped by planning how I would end it
It was brilliant for me as a kid when things were too bad to
cope with.
Why did no-one notice what was happening to me?
Why would no-one listen to me?

Why was I told it was wrong thinking?
That just made me feel even more crap about myself.
I'm glad that someone finally listened

I hope that it will help other people who are going through the
shit
to know you can escape.

There are other ways out.
There are people who will listen.

Being listened to was the most amazing thing that has ever
happened.
I have told my story so that you can understand a bit more
why sicko's like me think and act as we do.
Do not judge me.
You have not walked the path I have followed
I am glad that I'm alive now.
Are you?
I'm living.
Life's crap sometimes,
but it is all there is!

BIBLIOGRAPHY

Appelby, L., and R Warner. 1993. Parasuicide: Features of repetition and the implications for intervention. *Psychological medicine* 23:13-16.

Bachelard, G. 1964. *The poetics of space.* Edited by M. T. Jolas. New York: Orion Press.

BACP. 2009. Ethical framework for good practice in counselling and psychotherapy. Rugby: BACP.

Baraclough, B. 1987. *Suicide: Clinical and epidemiological.* New York: Croom Helm.

Baraclough, B, and D Pallis. 1975. Depression followed by suicide: a comparison of depressed suicides with living depressives. *Psychological medicine* 5:55-61.

Behan, C. 1999. Linking lives around shared themes: narrative group therapy with gay men. *Gecko: A journal of deconstruction and narrative ideas in therapeutic practice* vol.2.

Behan, C. 2003 *Rescued speech poems: co-authoring poetry in narrative therapy* accessed 15.5.07

Bird, J. 2000. *The Heart's Narrative:Therapy and navigating life's contradictions.* Green Bay Aukland: Edge Press

—. 2004. *Talk that sings.* Aukland: Edge Press.

Bond, T. 2000. *Standards and ethics for counselling.* London: Sage publications.

—. 2004. *Ethical guidelines for researching counselling and psychotherapy.* Rugby: British Association of Counselling and Psychotherapy.

Bowlby, J. 1982. *Attachment and Loss Vol 1.* New York: Pegasus Books.

Brown, GW, CJ Gollop, MG Goodson, P Green-Powell, A Hambrick, LA Kingham, J Moody, C Obbo, EA Peterson, DD Turner, KM Vaz, J Walcott-McQuigg, and RT White. 1997. *Oral narrative research with black women.* Edited by K. M. Vaz. London: Sage Publications.

Browne, A, and D Finkelhor. 1986. Impact of child sexual abuse a review of the research. *Psychological bulletin* 99 (1):66-77.

Chapman, T, K 2005 Expressions of "Voice" in Portraiture in *Qualitative Inquiry 2005* 11;27

Cixous, H., and M. Calle-Gruber. 1997. *Rootprints: memory and life writing*. London: Routledge.

Clough, P 2002. *Narratives and fictions in educational research*. Buckingham: Open University Press.

Collins, G. 1988. *Christian Counselling*. London: Word (UK) Ltd.

Dale, S. 1999. Our bones are dried up and our hope is gone: Unpublished dissertation submitted for Diploma in Pastoral Counselling Nottingham University.

—. 2003. Ethical implications for counsellors working with the suicidal: Unpublished paper submitted as coursework for Bristol University.

—. 2006. Where angels fear to tread: an exploration of the experience of having conversations about suicide in a counselling context. narrative inquiry, MSc Dissertation Graduate School of Education, Bristol University, Bristol.

DOH. 2002. National suicide prevention strategy for England, edited by D. o. Health: www.gov.uk.

Dorpat, T, and H Riley. 1960. A study of suicide in the Seattle area. *Comprehensive psychiatry* 1:349-359.

Egan, G. 1990 *The Skilled Helper (4th edition)*. Pacific Grove California: Brooks/Cole publishing company - a division of Wadsworth, Inc.

Ellis, C. 2007. Telling secrets, revealing lives: relational ethics in research with intimate others. *Qualitative Inquiry* 13 (3).

Ellis, C, and A Bochner. 1992. Telling and performing personal stories. In *Investigating subjectivity*, edited by C. Ellis and A. Bochner. London: sage publications.

Epston, D. 2004. From empathy to ethnography: the origin of therapeutic co research. *The international journal of narrative therapy and community work 2004* 2.

Erikson, E. 1982. *The life cycle completed: A review*. New York: Norton.

Etherington, K. 2000. *Narrative approaches to working with adult male survivors of child sexual abuse*. London: Jessica Kingsley publishers.

—. 2001. Research with ex-client's a celebration and extension of the therapeutic process. *British journal of guidance and counselling* 29 (1).

—. 2004. *Becoming a reflexive researcher: using ourselves in research*. London: Jessica Kingsley publishers.

—. 2007. Ethical Research in Reflexive Relationships. *Qualitative Inquiry* 13 (599).

Etkind, M. 1997. *...or not to be: a collection of suicide notes*. New York: Riverhead books The Berkeley Publishing Group.

Foucault, M. 1980. *Power/knowledge: selected interviews and other writings*. New York: Panthean books.

—. 1984. *The history of sexuality*. London: Panthean books.

Frank, A W. 1995. *The wounded storyteller: body, illness, and ethics,* . Chicago, IL: University of Chicago Press.

Freedman, J, and G Combs. 1996. *Narrative Therapy: the social construction of preferred realities*. New York: W.W. Norton Company Inc.

Goodwin, F.K., and K. R. Jamison. 1990. *Manic Depressive Illness*. New York: Oxford University Press.

Gov.UK. 2009 *Suicide Rates*. http://www.statistics.gov.uk/cci/nugget.asp?id=1092 accessed 22.11.09.

Greenspan, H. 2003. Listening to holocaust survivors: interpreting a repeated story. In *Up Close and Personal: The teaching and learning of narrative research*, edited by R. Josselson, A. Liebliech and D. P. McAdams. Washington: American Psychological Association.

Grove, D. J., and B.I. Panzer. 1991. *Resolving traumatic memories: metaphors and symbols in psychotherapy*. New York: Irvington Publishers, Inc.

Guze, S, and E Robins. 1970. Suicide and primary affective dissorder. *British Journal of Psychiatry* 117:437-438.

Harris, E.C., and B Baraclough. 1997. Suicide as an outcome for mental disorders: a meta-analysys. *British Journal of Psychiatry* 170:205-228.

Hart, N, and A Crawford-Wright. 1999. Research as therapy, therapy as research: ethical dilemmas in new-paradigm research. *British journal of guidance and counselling* Vol.27 (2).

Heckler, R A. 1994. *Waking up alive: the descent to suicide and return to life*. New York: G.P. Putmam's.

Hill, D, A. 2005. The poetry in portraiture: seeing subjects, hearing voices, and feeling contexts. *Qualitative Inquiry* 11.

Hooks, B. 1994. *Teaching to transgress*. New York: Routledge.

—. 1999. *Remembered rapture: the writer at work*. New York: Women's Press Ltd.

Houston, G. 1990. *Supervision and Counselling*. London: The Rochester Foundation.

Howe, D, M Brandon, D Hinings, and G Schofield. 1999. *Attachment theory, child maltreatment and family support*. Basingstoke: Macmillan press.

Hume. 2004. Suicide. *The Times 12th November 2004*.

Hutton, J. 2008. Turning the spotlight back on the normalising gaze. *International Journal of Narrative Therapy and Community Work* 1:3-16.

Jacobs, M. 1998. *The presenting past: the core of psychodynamic counselling and therapy second edition.* Buckingham: Open University Press.

Janesick, V. J. 1999. A Journal about journal writing as a qualitative research technique: history, issues, and reflections. *Qualitative Inquiry* 5 (4).

Jenkins, P. 2002. *Legal issues in counselling and psychotherapy.* Edited by T. Bond, *Ethics in practice.* London: Sage.

Josselson, R. 1996. *Ethics and process in the narrative study of lives.* Thousand Oaks. Sage.

Josselson, R, A Lieblich, and D P McAdams. 2003. *Up close and personal: the teaching and learning of narrative research.* Washington: American psychological association.

Kristeva, L., ed. 1974. *Revolution in poetic language.* Edited by K. Oliver, *The Portable Kristeva.* New York: Columbia University Press.

Langellier, K M. 2001. You're marked; breast cancer, tattoo, and the narrative performance of identity. In *Narrative and identity*, edited by J. Brockmeier and D. Carbaugh. Amsterdam: John Benjamins publishing company.

Lapadat, J.C. and Lindsay, A.C. 1999. Transcription in research and practice: from standardization of technique and interpretive positionings. In *Qualitative Inquiry* 5, 1, 64-86.

Law, F., X. Coll, A. Tobias, and K. Hawton. 1998. Child sexual abuse in women who take overdoses: II. Risk factors and associations. *Archives of suicide research* 4:307-327.

Lee, M. 1993. *Doing research on sensitive topics.* London: Sage publications.

Maris, R.F.W. 1991. Introduction to a special issue: Assessment and prediction of suicide. *Suicide and life-threatening behaviour* 21:1-17.

Marttunen, M.J, M.A. Hillevi, M.M Henriksson, and J.K. Lonnquist. 1991. Mental disorders in adolescent suicide. DSM-III-R Axes I and II diagnoses in suicides among 13 to 19 year olds in Finland. *Archives of general psychiatry* 48:834-839.

Maslow, A. H. 1968. *Towards a psychology of being.* New York: Van Nostrand Reinhold.

—. 1973. *The Farther Reaches of Human Nature.* Harmondsworth: Penguin.

McAdams, D P. 1993. *The stories we live by: personal myths and the making of the self.* New York: Guilford Press.

McLeod, J. 2006. Narrative thinking and the emergence of post-psychological therapies. *Narrative Inquiry* 16 (1):201-10.

Menninger, W. 1991. Patient suicide and its impact on the psychotherapist. *Bulletin of the Menninger Clinic* 55:216-227.

Morgan, H.G. 1993. Suicide Prevention: the assessment and management of suicide risk. Bristol: Health Advisory Service.

Myerhoff, B. 1979. *Number our days*. London. New York: Meridian published by Penguin group.

—. 1982. Life history among the elderly: Performance, visibility and remembering. In *A crack in the mirror: reflexive perspectives in anthropology*, edited by J. Ruby. Philadelphia: University of Pennsilvania.

—. 1986. Life not death in Venice: It's second life. In *The anthropology of experience*, edited by V. Turner and E. Bruner. Chicago: University of Illinois Press.

National, Collaborating, Centre for, and Mental Health. 2004. The Short-term physical and psychological management of secondary prevention of self-harm in primary and secondary care. Leicester: British Psychological Society.

O'Connor, J, and J Seymour. 1995. *Introducing NLP: Psychological skills for understanding and influencing people*. London: Thorsons an imprint of Harper Collins Publishers.

O'Connor, R, and N Sheehy. 2000. *Understanding suicidal behaviour*. London: British Psychological Association.

O'Neill, M. 2004. A conversation with Angela, Brett and Jess about suicidal thoughts, failure and resistance. *International Journal of Narrative Therapy and Community Work* 3:41-42.

—. 2004. Researching 'suicidal thoughts' and archiving young people's insider knowledges. *International Journal of Narrative Therapy and Community Work* 3:38-40.

Oritz, S. 2001. How interviewing became therapy for wives of professional athletes: learning from a serendipitous experience. *Qualitative Inquiry* 7 (2):192-221.

Parris, M. 2004. Suicide. *The Times*. 20.11.2004.

Pembroke, L.R., ed. 1996. *Self-Harm: Perspectives from personal experience, Survivors speak out*. London: Chipmunka Publishing.

Plath, S. 1981. *Sylvia Plath: Collected Poems*. London: Faber and Faber.

Pritichard, C. 1995. *Suicide: The ultimate rejection*. Buckingham: Open University Press.

Rayner, E. 1986. *Human Development (3rd edition)*. London: Routledge.

Reeves, A, and R Mintz. 2001. Counsellors' experiences of working with suicidal clients: an exploratory study: . *Counselling and Psychotherapy Research*, 1 (3):172-176.

Reeves, A, and P Seber. 2004. Working with the suicidal client. *Counselling and Psychotherapy Research,* 15 (4).

Richards, B. M. 2000. Impact upon therapy and the therapist when working with suicidal patients: some transference and countertransference aspects. *British Journal of Guidance and Counselling* 28 (3).

Richardson, L. 1990. *Writing strategies; reaching diverse audiences.* California: Sage publications.

—. 1992. The consequences of poetic representation: writing the other, re-writing the self. In *Investigating subjectivity: research on lived experience*, edited by C. a. F. Ellis, M. Newbury Park, CA: Sage.

—. 2000. Introduction- assessing alternative modes of qualitative and ethnographic research: how do we judge? Who judges? *Qualitative Inquiry* Vol 6 (2):251-252.

—. 2000. Writing: A method of Inquiry. In *Handbook of qualitative research*, edited by N. K. Denzien and Y. Lincoln. London: Sage Publications.

—. 2003. Poetic representation of interviews In *Postmodern Interviewing*, edited by J. Gubrium and J. Holstein. London: Sage.

Richardson, L , and E Adams St. Pierre. 2000. Writing a Method of Inquiry. In *Handbook of Qualitative Research*, edited by N. K. Denzin and Y. Lincoln. London: Sage.

Riessman, C, K. 2008. *Narrative methods for the human sciences.* London: Sage.

—. 2002. Doing justice: positioning the interpreter in narrative work. In *Strategic narrative: New perspectives on the power of personal and cultural stories*, edited by W. Patterson. Oxford: Lexington Books.

Robins, E, G Murphy, R Wilkinson, S Gassner, and J Kayes. 1959. Some clinical considerations in the prevention of suicide based on a study of 134 successful suicides. *American JOurnal of Public Health* 49:888-898.

Rogers, C. 1961. *On becoming a person.* London: Constable.

—. 1978. *On personal power.* London: Constable.

Rowan, J. 1983. *The Reality Game: a guide to humanistic counselling and psychotherapy.* London: Routledge.

Roy, A. 1982a. Risk factors for suicide in psychiatric patients. *Archives of general psychiatry* 39:1089-1095.

—. 1982b. Suicide in chronic schizophrenia. *British Journal of Psychiatry* 141:171-177.

Russel, D.W. 1989. Job stress, social support and burnout among counseling center staff. *Journal of counseling psychology* 36 (4):464-470.

Sainsbury, P. 1955. *Suicide in London*. London: Chapman and Hall.

Sen, S. 2005. An Evening Air (translated by the poet) www.userpages.umbc.ed accessed 29.5.05.

Serin, S. 1926. Une enquete medico-psychologique sur le suicide a Paris. *La presse medicale*, November:1404-1406.

Shneidman. 1993. Suicide as pschache: a clinical approach to self-destructive behaviour. *Journal of nervous and mental disease* 181 (3).

Spandler, H. 2003. *Who's hurting who (2nd reprint)*. Bristol: 42nd Street - community based mental health resource for young people.

Speedy. 2005. Writing as inquiry: some ideas and practices. *Counselling and psychotherapy research* 5 (1):65-73.

Speedy, J. 2004. Living a more peopled life: definitional ceremony as inquiry into therapy outcomes. *International Journal of Narrative Therapy and Community Work* 3:43-53.

—. 2005. Collective biography practices: collective writing with the unassuming geeks group. *British Journal of Psychotherapy Integration* 2 (2) 29-38.

—. 2005. Using poetic documents: an exploration of poststructuralist ideas and poetic practices in narrative therapy. *British Journal of Guidance and Counselling* 33 (3).

—. 2007. Constructing stories: narrative interviews and conversations with Donald. In *Narrative Inquiry in psychotherapy*, edited by S. J. Houndsmill: Palgrave Macmillan.

—. 2007. *Narrative Inquiry and Psychotherapy*. Houndsmill: Palgrave Macmillan.

Tantam, D, and J Whittaker. 1992. Personality disorders and self-wounding. *British Journal of Psychiatry* 161:451-464.

Tedlock, D. 1983. *The spoken word and the work of interpretation*. Philadelphia: University of Pensylvania.

Thorne, B. 1991. *Person Centred Counselling*. London: Whur Publishers.

Trowner, P , A Casey, and W Dryden. 1988. *Cognitive Behavioural Counselling in Action*. Edited by W. Dryden. London: Sage Publications.

White, M. 1985. Fear busting and monster training. *Dulwich Centre Review* (1985).

—. 1995. *Re-Authoring Lives*. Adelaide: Dulwich Centre.

—. 1999. Different sources of power. Adelaide.

—. 2000. Reflecting teamwork as definitional ceremony re-visited. In *Reflections on narrative practice: essays and interviews*, edited by M. White. Adelaide: Dulwich Publications.

—. 2001. Narrative practice and the unpacking of identity conclusions. *Gecko: A journal of deconstruction and narrative practice* 2001 (1).

—. 2002. Workshop notes. *articles.* Adelaide: Dulwich Centre http://www.dulwichcentre.com.au accessed 12.4.03.

—. 2003. Definitional ceremony and outsider witness responses. In *narrative therapy and community work conference.* Adelaide: Dulwich Centre http://www.dulwichcentre.com.au accessed 30.5.07.

—. 2003. Narrative practice and community assignments. *International Journal of Narrative Therapy and Community Work* 2.

—. 2004. *Resurrecting diversity in everyday life.* Adelaide: Dulwich Centre Publications.

—. 2007. Working with trauma. Paper read at International Conference of Narrative Therapy and Community Work, at Norway.

White, M , and D Epston. 1990. *Narrative means to therapeutic ends.* New York: W.W. Norton and company.

Williams, G. 1984. The genesis of chronic illness: narrative re-construction. *Sociology of Health and Illness* 6:175-200.

Williams, M. 1922. *The original velveteen rabbit.* London: Mamoth, an imprint of Reed Books Ltd.

Williams, Mark. 1997. *Cry of Pain: Understanding suicide and self-harm.* London: Penguin.

Winter, D., S. Bradshaw, F. Bunn, and D. Wellsted. 2009. Counselling and psychotherapy for the prevention of suicide: a systematic review of the evidence. Lutterworth: British Association of Counselling and Psychotherapy (BACP)

Wosket, V. 1999. *The therapeutic use of self.* London: Routledge.

INDEX

abandoned, 118, 121
abuse, 105, 123
abused, 44
abusive, 112, 114, 139
abandonment, 90
academia, 42
academic, 57, 61, 149, 150, 161
acceptance, 11
accepted, 109
accountability, 21 ,22, 25, 136, 139
accountable, 21, 45
act of resistance, 61
afraid, 91, 92
addicted,
alcohol, 11, 41
alcoholism, 27
alive, 78, 99, 100, 162
alone, 98, 106, 121, 131
alternatives, 123
alternative stories, 117, 154, 164
ambivalent, 35, 72, 89
anger, 90, 105, 143
angry, 74, 82, 86, 99, 105, 108,
    109,142,143
anguish, 92
anonymity, 37, 89
anonymous, 38, 85
anxiety, 34
ashamed, 74, 75, 82, 86, 109
assumptions, 35, 150
attachment theories, 11
audience, 12
autonomy, 32, 35, 44, 45, 166
BACP, 25, 32, 166
balance of power, 49
battle, 48, 159
beams, 81, 166
boundaries, 18, 72, 141
breach of confidence, 33

burial service, 29
calm, 102, 145
challenge, 126, 153
chaos, 9, 72, 73, 94, 107
child, 140
childhood, 98, 115
childhood abuse, 11, 27, 110
childhood trauma, 11
choices, 120, 127
client autonomy, 32
client centred, 43
client rights, 25, 34
codes of practice, 31
cognitive behavioural theories, 11
collaboration, 154
collaborative, 63, 120, 146, 163
collective, 51, 132, 146
commitment, 142
community, 17, 137
confidentiality, 32, 35, 102
congruent, 19
connected, 131, 136
connecting, 145
consequences, 36, 136, 140, 145
consulting with my consultants, 20
control, 39, 42, 45, 46, 47, 48, 54,
    68, 70, 102, 111, 114, 115, 122,
    125, 164
core conditions, 11
CORE, 153
co-research, 15, 68
co-researcher, 12, 13, 19, 21, 45, 50
counselling research, 15
counsellor perspectives, 25
cowardly betrayal, 29
criminal status, 28
cultural, 16
de-centre, 49

definitional ceremony, 3, 93, 131,
    132, 133, 134, 135, 136, 137,
    148, 164
depressed, 27, 89
depression, 33, 34, 164
depressive illness, 27
de-skilled, 97, 104
despair, 50, 72, 90, 97, 105, 113,
    148, 161
desperation, 33, 143
destroy, 109, 110
diagnosis, 43, 101
different choices, 47
disempowered, 44, 45
disrespectful, 21
drug misuse, 41
drugs, 11
dual relationships, 18, 19, 20, 22
dying, 117, 118, 120
ECT, 47
emotional blackmail, 113
emotive, 28
empathy, 11
empowered, 22, 45, 49
ending, 134, 135
endurance, 107
escape, 103, 110, 115, 123
escaping, 125
ethical, 18, 63, 117, 120, 133, 141,
    148, 152
ethical challenges, 2, 32, 34
ethical decision making, 163
ethical dilemmas, 1, 25, 26, 36, 57,
    136
ethical framework, 26, 32
ethical guidelines, 31
ethical implications, 90, 102
ethical mindfulness, 21, 23, 154
ethical principles, 15, 20
ethical responsibility, 16
ethical values, 32
ethically challenging,
ethically mindful, 16
ethics, 31, 162
evidence led, 43
expectations, 41

expert, 49, 68
expert knowledge, 51
expert witness, 21
exposed, 108
externalised, 13
failing as a suicide, 44, 103
fault, 82
fear, 49, 142, 145
fictionalised stories, 21
for Gods sake get a grip, 83, 92
freedom, 48
frustration, 94
funeral, 98
gaps and cracks, 50, 123
grief, 90
grieving, 117
guilt, 70, 127
guilty, 40
guidelines, 22, 35
hate, 75, 81, 110, 158
hating, 73
helpless, 97, 104
helplessness, 30
historical factors, 29
hope, 137, 138, 154
hopelessness, 97
horror, 28
humanistic, 11
humiliating, 77
humiliation, 73, 82
identities, 18, 49
identity, 13, 15, 4, 50, 53, 84, 133
individual experience, 17
invisible, 76, 78, 132
isolated, 104, 118, 132, 132, 136,
    143, 146, 148
isolation, 27, 114, 124, 143, 154,
    163
judge, 167
judged, 127
judgment, 86
judgmental, 29
knife throwers assistant, 100
knowledge, 39, 42, 45, 46, 49, 50,
    56, 68, 147, 154, 161
language, 56

law, 31, 33
laugh, 108
laughter, 103, 115, 126,
liberating, 76, 77
life. 34, 102, 104, 155
litigation, 139, 148
lives linked round common themes,
    51
living, 147
living alone, 27
loneliness, 112
loss, 107
low self esteem, 27
madness, 80
malpractice, 148
manipulatively, 114
marginalised, 14, 44, 57, 62, 150
margins of society, 18
meaningless, 106
medical negligence, 29
memories, 11, 85, 124
mental health, 14, 17, 27, 41, 48, 50,
    101, 163
Mental Health Act 1983, 32
metaphor, 132
methodology, 55
modern power, 42
moral attitudes, 29
moral code, 162
moral judgement, 43
mortal sin, 90
multi-layered narrative, 62
narrative inquiry, 14
narrative therapy, 14, 19
Neuro Linguistic Programming, 11
NICE, 26
non-judgmental, 36, 163
normalising judgements, 43, 44
normalization, 51
obligations, 22
oblivion, 70, 100, 167
oral narratives, 61
out of control, 67, 69
outsider witnesses, 92, 135, 136
pain, 93, 96, 98, 99, 100, 104, 115,
    160, 161

panic, 26, 30, 101,140
participants, 55
peace, 69
peaceful, 59, 60, 96, 98
personality disorder, 27, 163, 164
personal moral qualities, 32
planning, 93, 96, 125
poem, 85
poetic, 14, 22, 57, 60
poetic narrative, 22
poetry, 61
possibilities, 34
power, 39, 40, 41, 44, 45, 46,47, 48,
    49, 50, 120, 134, 148, 159, 160
power dynamic, 37, 45
power imbalance, 22
power of breath, 68
power of personal stories, 50
power struggle, 48
power systems, 45
powerful, 48, 74, 78, 106, 143
preferred position, 144
preferred reality, 10
prescription drugs, 70
prejudices, 30
principles, 32
privacy, 37
private, 158
process of becoming, 18
professional responsibilities, 25
protect, 92
psychiatric care, 9
psychiatry, 30
psychodynamic, 11
psychological perspectives, 29
punishing, 96
purpose, 19, 20
quantitative research, 16
rape, 45
raped, 109, 115
real, 100, 114, 124, 125
real self, 11
re-author, 13
re-authored, 49
re-connected, 148
reflect, 133, 156, 157

reflexive, 16, 17
reflexivity, 16
rejection, 90
relational, 17
research dilemmas, 22
research relationship, 17
resonate, 131, 136
resonating themes, 136
respect, 35, 36, 127, 157
respected, 160
responsibilities, 25, 30, 34, 68, 102
responsibility, 21, 31, 73, 84, 141
responsible, 37
re-telling, 60, 132, 133, 136
return to life, 104
risk, 18, 33, 146, 153, 164
role reversal, 37
rope, 101, 102
sad, 86, 118
sadness, 90
safe, 35, 68
safety, 35, 38
scared, 91, 109, 111, 115, 118, 119,
    124, 127, 139
schizophrenia, 27, 164
secondary traumatisation, 166
secrecy, 40, 132
secret, 72, 119, 120
self-awareness, 163
self-destructive, 33, 110, 123
self-disclosure, 22
self-harm, 11
self-hate, 80, 109
self-help, 72
severe mood disorders, 27
sexual abuse, 40
shame, 86, 97
side-stepping, 47, 48, 50
silenced, 131
silences, 5, 90
silent, 89
social attitudes, 43
social behaviour, 61
social construction, 2, 10
social support, 27
socially construct, 15, 17

socially constructed, 10, 13,14
socially isolated, 27
spiritual, 71, 140
stanza, 22, 62,136
statistics, 152, 153
staying with, 136, 137, 139, 141,
    148
strength, 126
stress, 72
stressful, 152
structuralist, 12
substance abuse, 27
suicidal trance, 104
suicide prevention, 18, 43, 155, 165
supervision, 117, 162, 166
supervisor, 26, 121, 122,163
survive, 119, 126
survived, 99
taboo, 28, 62, 84, 146
talk that sings, 58
tears, 94, 157
terrified, 122
terrifying, 48, 126
therapeutic, 16, 17, 62
therapeutic relationships, 10
thickening, 51
thicker richer descriptions, 12, 62
threshold spaces, 50
traditional power, 42, 49
transcribe, 148
transcribing, 57
transcription, 59, 60
transparent, 62, 63
transparently, 22
trapped, 34, 67, 79, 120, 122, 144,
    159, 161
traumatic, 90
trust, 5, 20, 100, 109, 110
trusting, 140
trustworthiness, 20
truth, 17, 53, 56, 154
ultimate control, 154
ultimate rejection, 31
ultimate solution, 28
unassuming geeks, 30, 68
unconditional positive regard, 11

unemployed, 27
useless, 97
vicarious trauma, 144
voice, 57
vulnerabilities, 38
vulnerable, 21, 37, 45, 72, 108, 118,
    164

witness, 104
witnesses, 132, 134, 146, 164
wobbliness, 31, 37, 38, 84
writing, 55, 57, 158
writing up, 55
wrong thinking, 14, 43, 47, 80, 118,
    127, 164, 165, 167